After Stagflation

After Stagflation

Alternatives to economic decline

Edited by
JOHN CORNWALL

M. E. SHARPE, INC
Armonk, New York

© Basil Blackwell, 1984

First published in 1984 by M. E. Sharpe, Inc.,
80 Business Park Drive, Armonk, New York 10504

All rights reserved. Except for the quotation of short passages for the purpose of criticism and review, no part of this publication may be reproduced, stored in a retrieval system, or transmitted, in any form or by any means, electronic, mechanical, photocopying, recording or otherwise, without the prior written permission of M. E. SHARPE, INC.

Library of Congress Cataloging in Publication Data

Main entry under title:

After stagflation.

   Includes index.
   1. Economic policy – Addresses, essays, lectures.
2. Unemployment – Effect of inflation on – Addresses, essays, lectures.   3. Capitalism – Addresses, essays, lectures.
4. Economic history – 1971–   – Addresses, essays, lectures.   I. Cornwall, John.
HD88.A35   1984   338.9   83–27140
ISBN 0–87332–271–3

Printed and bound in Great Britain

Contents

List of Contributors		vii
Preface		ix
1	Introduction *John Cornwall*	1
2	After Disinflation, Then What? *James Tobin*	20
3	After Monetarism *Richard G. Lipsey*	41
4	Confusion in Economic Theory and Policy – Is There a Way Out? *Wynne Godley*	63
5	Stagflation as an Issue of Economic Policy *Erik Lundberg*	86
6	The Phyrric Victory – Unemployment, Inflation and Macroeconomic Policy *Lars Osberg*	111
7	International Aspects of Stagflation *A. M. Sinclair*	133
8	The Implications of an Inflationary Bias *John Cornwall*	157
Author Index		178
Subject Index		179

List of Contributors

John Cornwall is Professor of Economics at Dalhousie University. His most recent book is *Conditions for Economic Recovery: A Post-Keynesian Analysis*.

Wynne Godley is Professor of Economics at Cambridge University and Director of the Department of Applied Economics. He is co-author of the recently published *Macroeconomics*.

Richard Lipsey is the Sir Edward Peacock Professor of Economics at Queen's University. He is the author of numerous books and articles and a past president of the Canadian Economic Association.

Erik Lundberg is Professor Emeritus at the Stockholm School of Economics. The author of many books and articles, he is a past President of the Swedish Economic Association and a member of the Nobel Prize Selection Committee in Economics.

Lars Osberg is Associate Professor of Economics at Dalhousie University and specializes in Labour Economics. He is the author of the recently published *Economic Inequality in America*.

Alasdair Sinclair is Professor of Economics and currently Academic Vice-President at Dalhousie. His research has been in the areas of International Trade and Economic History.

James Tobin is Sterling Professor of Economics at Yale University. In 1981 he was awarded the Nobel Prize in Economics. He served as president of the Econometric Society in 1958 and the American Economic Association in 1971.

Preface

The Dorothy J. Killam Memorial Lectures were established at Dalhousie University in Halifax, Nova Scotia to honour Mrs Killam for her generosity to the University. In the Autumn of 1982, the ninth anniversary of the Lectures, four outstanding economists — Wynne Godley, Richard Lipsey, Eric Lundberg and James Tobin — took part in the lecture series. Each was asked to speak on the topic of whether there were alternatives to the economic decline that had overtaken the developed capitalist economies in recent times.

The Dalhousie community was not just treated to four original and thoughtful public addresses. Each of the invited guest speakers agreed to participate in an informal seminar focusing on the current policies of their respective countries. 'Reaganism', and 'Thatcherism', together with current economic problems in Canada and Sweden, were given a thorough hearing. For anyone seriously interested in the current economic difficulties, it was a most enlightening and rewarding period.

When I first approached each of the speakers, it was very much in my mind to have the lectures published as the core of a book that would give a non-monetarist, non-Marxist analysis of today's major economic problems, together with policy recommendations. Each one agreed to my proposal and their papers make up the first part of the book. In spite of the inevitable time lapse between the completion of the papers and their publication, they remain as fresh as ever.

Two members of the Economics Faculty at Dalhousie, Lars Osberg and Alasdair Sinclair, were also asked to contribute papers. These are included along with an introduction and a contribution by myself. Various aspects of the stagflation problem are taken up. The general tone of the papers ranges from pessimism to optimism in our ability to realize something better than the dismal conditions of the last decade. The reader should find the papers very helpful in understanding the central issues of the policy debates on inflation, stagnation and unemployment.

I would like to take this opportunity to thank Dr W. A. MacKay, President of Dalhousie, and Dr Kenneth Leffek, Dean of the Graduate School at Dalhousie, for their assistance and encouragement throughout the various stages of the Lectures and the putting together of this 'Dalhousie statement'.

1
Introduction
JOHN CORNWALL*

BACKGROUND

The inflation record

The quarter of a century following the reconversion from the Second World War, roughly the early 1950s until 1973 or 1974, marks the 'golden age' of capitalism. In no other period did so many capitalist economies grow so rapidly for such an extended period of time. Rates of growth of labour productivity and per capita incomes reached historical highs in almost all of the developed capitalist economies, the USA being the notable exception. Unemployment rates fell to historical lows and, for the first 20 years of the period at least, inflation rates were tolerable if not acceptable.

Looking back, it is clear the late 1960s marked the beginning of the end of this remarkable era. Consider the data in Table 1.1 in which average rates of price inflation are given for selective periods for the seven largest OECD countries. The period 1955–65 was one of more-or-less steady, slow increase in rates of inflation within that decade. The 1966–70 period marked the first noticeable acceleration of inflation rates in many countries. By 1973 this had become a universal phenomenon and by 1974 inflation rates had roughly doubled their 1973 rates in a large number of economies.

Restrictive policies were put into effect in most countries by 1974 to reduce inflation. In most countries there was a sharp decline in inflation rates by 1976 or 1977 but as Table 1.1 reveals, taking the period from 1975–79 as a whole, little headway was made in reducing inflation outside of Japan and Germany. Even here, however, inflation rates seem to have got 'stuck' at relatively

---

* I should like to acknowledge the helpful comments and criticisms of Wendy Maclean.

Table 1.1 Average rates of increase of consumer prices in seven countries, selected periods

	Canada (%)	France (%)	Italy (%)	Japan (%)	UK (%)	USA (%)	West Germany (%)
1955–65	1.6	4.4	3.3	3.3	2.9	1.5	2.3
1966–70	3.9	4.4	3.0	5.4	4.6	4.2	2.4
1971–72	3.8	5.9	5.4	5.3	8.4	3.8	5.5
1973–74	9.2	10.6	15.0	18.1	12.6	8.6	7.0
1975–79	8.9	10.1	15.5	7.3	15.7	8.1	4.1
1980–81	11.3	13.5	20.0	6.5	15.0	12.0	5.7
1982	10.8	12.1	16.5	2.6	8.6	6.2	5.3

Source: IMF *International Financial Statistics*, Supplement in Price Adjustment, 1981 and 1982.

high levels. Including the smaller OECD countries would not alter the picture. Comparing the 1955–65 period with 1975–9, rates of inflation showed a definite tendency to ratchet upward (and at a time when unemployment rates also moved upward) even before the full force of the second oil-price rise was felt. The marked acceleration of inflation rates in 1980–1 (outside Japan) reflects this 'shock' and some of its after effects. Only in 1982 do inflation rates begin to come down noticeably.

The impact of restrictive policies

What caused the acceleration beginning in the late 1960s and what kept inflation rates high until very recently are matters of dispute. What is not open to question was the reaction of the various governments to the inflation, an intensification of restrictive policies. This became most apparent during the downturn of 1973–4. Rather than intervene actively with stimulative policies once it became clear that unemployment rates were going to rise, one government after another allowed the recession to grow worse in hopes that a policy-induced or advanced recession would bring down inflation rates. Balance-of-payments difficulties arising out of the OPEC oil-price increases provided additional reasons for restrictive measures.

Table 1.2 gives unemployment figures for the same seven OECD countries. The 1966–73 averages are shown along with annual figures beginning in 1974. A steady upward trend in unemployment

Table 1.2 Standardized unemployment rates in the seven large OECD economics, 1966–82

	Canada (%)	France* (%)	West Germany (%)	Italy (%)	Japan (%)	UK* (%)	USA (%)
1966–73	5.2	2.2	0.9	5.7	1.2	3.3	4.4
1974	5.3	2.8	1.6	5.3	1.4	3.2	5.5
1975	6.9	4.1	3.6	5.8	1.9	4.7	8.3
1976	7.1	4.4	3.7	6.6	2.0	6.0	7.5
1977	8.0	4.7	3.6	7.0	2.0	6.3	6.9
1978	8.3	5.2	3.5	7.1	2.2	6.3	5.9
1979	7.4	5.9	3.2	7.5	2.1	5.6	5.7
1980	7.5	6.3	3.0	7.4	2.0	7.0	7.0
1981	7.5	7.3	4.4	8.3	2.2	10.7	7.5
1982	10.9	8.0	6.1	8.9	2.4	12.5	9.5

Source: *Economic Outlook*, July, 1981, December, 1982, and July, 1983, Table R12.
* Series adjusted by OECD.

rates is discernible in all seven countries. Whatever reversal can be found was of minor consequence. For example, unemployment rates fell slightly during the mini-boom of the late 1970s in both Germany and the United States. Even so, unemployment rates of 3.2 and 5.7 per cent in 1979 in Germany and the United States, respectively, must be compared to the unemployment highs of 1.3 per cent in 1967 in Germany and 5.8 in 1971 in the United States in the 1966–73 period.

Unless one is prepared to argue that rising unemployment rates primarily reflect an increased desire for leisure, the Keynesian impact of aggregate demand on unemployment is clear from Table 1.2. Restrictive aggregate demand policies can noticably affect the real sector. Comparing Tables 1.1 and 1.2 also indicates how difficult it is to get inflation out of a system once it is firmly embedded. Even though unemployment rates stabilized at post-war highs or even increased from 1975 to 1979, rates of inflation if anything accelerated. This remains true despite the fact that most of the impact of the second oil-price shock was yet to come.

What also becomes clear is the association of depressed demand conditions with low productivity growth. Annual average rates of unemployment during 1963–73 and 1974–81 are given in Table 1.3 along with the annual average rates of growth of labour

Table 1.3 Rates of growth of labour productivity ($\dot{p}$) and average unemployment rates (u) for seven countries 1963–73 and 1974–81

	$\dot{p}$ (%)	u* (%)		$\dot{p}$ (%)	u* (%)
Canada			Britain		
1963–73	2.4	4.8	1963–73	3.0	3.2
1974–81	0.1	7.2	1974–81	0.8	6.2
France			United States		
1963–73	4.6	2.3	1963–73	1.9	4.3
1974–81	2.3	5.1	1974–81	0.0	6.8
Italy			West Germany		
1963–73	5.4	5.6	1963–73	4.6	0.8
1974–81	0.9	6.9	1974–81	2.5	3.4
Japan					
1963–73	8.7	1.2			
1974–81	3.3	1.9			

Source: *Economic Outlook*, OECD, Paris, July, 1976, Table 13, December, 1981, Tables 5 and R12, and December, 1982 Tables 14 and R12.
* 1965–73.

productivity for the seven largest OECD economies. A strong negative correlation holds for all countries, strongly suggesting that the current stagnation in growth rates is at least partly related to the depressed demand conditions.

WHAT WENT WRONG?

Comparing the periods from the early 1870s until the mid to late 1880s, the decade before the turn of the century until the First World War and the post-war period until very recently, a distinct upward trend in the rates of wage and price inflation is evident in capitalist countries for which there is continuous data. In the first period, the rate of price inflation was negligible or even negative with the rate of wage inflation exceeded by rate of growth of productivity. The period from the mid to late 1880s up until 1913 saw a positive but very slight rate of price inflation as wage increases outstripped productivity growth. Compared to both periods the post-war period showed a marked increase in the rates of inflation of wages and prices. As just seen, within the post-war period there was a marked acceleration of inflation rates in almost all the developed capitalist economies. Only by 1982 is there any noticeable decline in the rates of inflation of either wages and prices.

The long-run upward trend beginning over 100 years ago in rates of wage and price inflation is a phenomenon demanding explanation in its own right. It is, however, the unusual developments beginning in the second half of the 1960s and lasting until very recently that are of chief concern to economists today. Three questions arise. First, why did inflation rates accelerate so dramatically during the latter part of the 1960s until approximately the middle of the 1970s? Secondly, why did inflation rates remain so high in the late 1970s compared, say to 1955–65, long after efforts to reduce inflation were implemented and before the second oil-price rise? Thirdly, what will happen if and when inflation rates have been brought down sufficiently to cause the authorities to begin doing something about reducing unemployment?

The second question can be reformulated. Why have efforts to reduce inflation rates been so costly in terms of unemployment and reduced economic growth? Note that the answer to this question provides the explanation of stagflation, the simultaneous occurance of high (and even rising) rates of inflation, and high and rising rates of unemployment and low growth.

What these questions point to is a serious malfunctioning of the developed capitalist systems. A period stretching over almost two decades has seen first a marked acceleration of inflation rates, followed by stagflation, and then rising unemployment rates and continued low growth with few indications of a return to conditions of the 1950s or early 1960s. While unemployment rates today are nowhere yet as bad as the 1930s, a record of high and even double-digit unemployment rates possibly stretching from one decade to the next is scant improvement over the record of the 1930s.

Such a serious breakdown of the modern capitalist economies, one becoming more evident over time, demands a serious explanation. Unfortunately, there are conflicting explanations and widely different policy prescriptions. The papers in this volume attempt to throw light on various aspects of this dismal situation. They have been written by an international group of economists from Europe and North America. The Lipsey and Tobin papers focus on the English-speaking countries while Lundberg's main concern is Sweden and other small, open economies. Nevertheless all of the papers deal with matters of relevance and concern for any of the developed capitalist economies. While there are important differences in the views taken here, there is much in the way of agreement, especially when these views are contrasted with other explanations of the origins and the forces behind the current difficulties. In this respect it is helpful to group explanations of recent events into three separate categories, the monetarist, the mainstream and post-Keynesian. A brief summary of these three positions together with their answers to the three questions just posed will place the papers to follow in a broader perspective.

ALTERNATIVE EXPLANATIONS OF THE RECENT PERFORMANCE

The monetarist explanation

Monetarism is the application of neoclassical precepts to the problems of inflation and unemployment. It is based on the standard, economics textbook view of markets in which price changes, including wages, reflect shifting demand and supply curves. Trading always takes place at intersection points or 'markets always clear'. If prices on average are rising it is because demand curves on average are shifting upward to the right. Ultimately, this can be traced to an increase in the rate of growth of the money supply. Inflation is demand-pull and is always and everywhere a monetary phenomenon. Symmetry is a critical part of monetarist analysis also. The way to reduce prices is to reduce the rate of growth of the money supply. Demand curves will then shift downward to the left and, since markets always clear, prices will fall.

The modern version of monetarism has attempted to make this process more explicit and consistent with observed events. In doing so it has placed great emphasis on expectations, arguing that actual rates of inflation are also a function of expected rates of inflation. In this way, the persistence of inflation in spite of restrictive monetary measures can be explained. If reduction in the rate of growth of the money supply does not quickly affect actual rates of inflation, it is because expected rates of inflation are slow to adjust. People act on the basis of their expectations and only when they expect inflation rates to fall will they act in such a way that these expectations are fulfilled.

High and rising rates of unemployment can also persist but in the monetarist scheme they do not reflect deficiencies in aggregate demand, job offers and vacancies. Unemployment is either 'structural', e.g. due to market imperfections such as unions and minimum wage legislation, or voluntary and 'frictional' with people quitting existing jobs to search for better ones.[1] In this second case, unemployment reflects false perceptions of what can be gained or lost by being unemployed and searching for a better job. In the final analysis unemployment is largely if not totally voluntary and costless, an argument supposedly given added force by the increased importance in the post-war period of unemployment benefit schemes. Thirty-five million workers in the OECD are now undertaking a 'purposive quest for self-improvement' according to this view.

A corollary of this belief in the voluntary nature of unemployment is that a capitalist economy is self-regulating. Provided only that the authorities fix the rate of growth of the money supply, the economy will settle down at the 'natural rate of unemployment', a situation in which unemployment is voluntary and the rate of inflation is non-accelerating. There is no role for Keynesian demand-management policies. Furthermore, once the authorities learn to behave stagnation will end also and economic growth resume.

In the monetarist's view of events, the acceleration of inflation rates in so many countries in the late 1960s to early 1970s is explained simply in terms of the acceleration of rates of growth of the money supply, ultimately traced to growth of the money supply in the United States. International economic linkages have developed because of the increased international interdependence of trading countries. As a result any acceleration of the rate of growth of the money supply in a large economy such as the United States is quickly transmitted to the rest of the world in the form of a higher rate of growth of central bank reserves in other countries. This is followed by a more rapid rate of growth of their money supplies and, ultimately, prices.

The persistance of high rates of inflation after 1974 in spite of efforts to restrict the rate of growth of the money supply is alternatively explained in terms of the slowness of people to change their expectations about inflation, and hence to act upon expectations more conducive to reducing actual rates, or a failure of the authorities to actually reduce the rate of growth of the money supply. Both explanations have been extended by monetarists with an influential notion, 'credibility'. The failure of policy to be credible, i.e. the failure of the monetary authorities to so convince the public that it is serious about its efforts to reduce inflation, is seen as the source of the failure to reduce inflation quickly and dramatically. Credibility must be achieved by a rapid decrease in the rate of growth of the money supply and public announcements that such restrictive policies will be enforced until inflation comes down.

The 'mainstream' explanation of recent events[2]

Monetarism, based as it is on the neoclassical view of markets, has little regard for the importance of institutions in its explanation of recent events. The economy is one of atomistic competition or, if the existence of unions and oligopolies is recognized, the market system still performs 'as if' market power is not in evidence. Hence, the disregard for even a changing institutional framework.

A more widely acceptable explanation of today's events (at least outside the United States) takes into account the importance of institutions and institutional change. Today's world of powerful corporations and unions, according to this view, is one of institutions that yield market and political power on a wide scale. This affects not only the way in which markets work but it substantially alters the nature of the inflationary process. Thus, there may be demand-pull forces at work in markets in which price changes reflect shifting demand and supply curves ('flex-price' markets), but in most markets prices, including wages, are determined as a mark-up over costs or are influenced by non-market forces ('fix-price' markets). This involves a mark-up over 'normal' unit costs in the case of product markets and the cost of living in the case of labour markets, together with a relative wage influence. As a result inflation is to a large extent cost-push in which a wage-price and a wage-wage mechanism generate a form of inflation that can take on a life of its own. Restrictive demand measures must be pronounced and prolonged in order to bring inflation down noticeably.

Following Keynes, this body of analysis recognizes basic asymmetries in the response of wages and prices (but not necessarily output and employment) to changes in aggregate demand. Increases in aggregate demand give rise to increases in rates of inflation that are greater than the impact of comparable decreases in demand on declines in rates of inflation.

Related to these arguments are the causes and nature of unemployment. When in fact the response of wages and prices to decreases in demand are moderate, quantity responses will be large. Output is cut back in product markets and employment in labour markets. When aggregate demand declines this gives rise to involuntary unemployment and the costs are large. Furthermore, as Keynes indicated 50 years ago, full employment will then involve active government intervention through fiscal and monetary policy. The economy is not self-regulating as it is in a monetarist-neoclassical world.

In the mainstream theory of inflation and unemployment, the inflationary mechanism can be activated and inflation rates accelerate for any number of reasons. Changes in the rate of growth of the money supply is only one possibility. Moreover such changes are often seen as effects rather than causes of inflation. For example, the acceleration of inflation rates in the 1960s has been attributed to a wage explosion in Europe little related to the state of the labour market, and to excess aggregate demand pressures in the United States connected with the Vietnam war. These influences activated the cost-push mechanisms just described causing inflation to accelerate. This was later reinforced by disturbances such as those coming from international commodity markets and OPEC which then fed into and kept the cost-push mechanisms going. In many cases the rate of growth of the money supply then adjusted to validate the on-going inflation.

The failure of restrictive policies to substantially reduce inflation rates for almost a decade can, according to this eclectic view, be attributed to several factors. The persistance of inflationary expectations, the favourite monetarist explanation, as an important inertial factor has been accepted by many non-monetarists. But the stress on institutional factors, fix-price markets and wage-wage and wage-price inflationary processes, leads straight to the conclusion that the labour market is in a constant state of disequilibrium. As a result current wage settlements will be strongly influenced by past events such as disturbances of the relative wage structure and efforts to re-establish or increase real wages through accelerated money wage demands. This has greatly lessened the impact of restrictive demand policies in bringing down wage and price inflation in the post-war period.

However, this position would admit that if sustained and strong enough, restrictive policies will eventually bring down inflation, although the cost in terms of involuntary unemployment is generally recognized to be very great. The credibility of policy has a role to play in the mainstream as well as the monetarist analysis of inflation. For example, by 1982 inflation rates began to fall noticeably in the OECD economies after almost a decade of restrictive policies, while unemployment rates soared. Many non-monetarist economists argue that only recently was policy strong enough to affect expectations and behaviour and thus bring down inflation.

A post-Keynesian view[3]

The failure of restrictive policies to sharply and quickly bring down inflation rates has been largely responsible for the development of a very pessimistic third view. This hold that full employment and price stability are no longer compatible unless collective bargaining settlements are made consistent on a continuous basis with price and wage stability, i.e. unless some kind of permanent incomes policy is adopted.

Consider the following argument. Assume that current restrictive policies succeed in bringing inflation rates down to a rate that is considered acceptable in the long-run. Because of the high costs of this policy in terms of unemployment, the authorities then wish to restimulate the economy and return to full employment. The critical question is: Will inflation rates begin to accelerate once full employment is attained or even earlier? A yes answer asserts the inability of the authorities to ever devise credible restrictive policies. Restrictive policies are capable of bringing down inflation through high rates of unemployment, but they are not enough to then allow a return to full employment without re-igniting serious inflation.

This pessimistic position argues that unfortunately the answer to the question is yes. The reasons for this lie in the same kinds of structural and institutional changes stressed by the mainstream group, e.g. the rise in unions and oligopolies and cost-push mechanisms, but this view asserts that periods of sustained full employment make the inflationary process explosive upwards. What is critical in the post-Keynesian position is a belief that what has developed in modern full employment, capitalist societies is a very noticeable inflationary bias; inflation rates tend to accelerate upwards under full employment or near full employ-

Introduction

ment conditions. To put it otherwise, the rate of unemployment at which inflation is constant or non-accelerating, the NAIRU, has increased and is only consistent with large amounts of involuntary unemployment.

The pessimist's explanation of recent events differs only slightly from the mainstream interpretation. A series of shocks, highly concentrated within a short span of time, activated the cost-push mechanisms in the various countries and their cumulative nature added a sustaining force to the inflationary process. The inability of restrictive policies to quickly and costlessly reduce inflation would also be very similar to the explanation given by mainstream economists and requires no further comment. However, post-Keynesian and mainstream economists differ in their attitudes as to whether the marked acceleration of inflation of the late 1960s to early 1970s was merely the result of the simultaneous occurrence of several adverse shocks that are not likely to be ever repeated or something more basic.

By the late 1960s, according to the post-Keynesian interpretation, the cost-push mechanisms had developed a strong, explosive, internal dynamic of their own, such that disturbances of any sort were capable of setting off accelerating inflationary processes. The most disturbing implication, naturally, is that restrictive demand policies can only bring temporary results. Even if they succeed in bringing down inflation, any subsequent restimulation of the economy merely recreates the potentially explosive conditions of the late 1960s.

THE IMPLICATIONS FOR POLICY

Monetarist policy

Expectedly, the different views on the nature of the current inflation (and stagnation) generate vastly different policy responses. The monetarist response is the most straight-forward and the simplest. By adhering to a policy of restricted growth of the money supply and, therefore, restricted aggregate demand, sooner or later expected rates of inflation will decline and bring down the actual rate of inflation in a mutual cause-and-effect process. The more credible is policy the sooner will policies succeed. The central banks need only show a little backbone and persistence. Furthermore, once inflation has been wrung out of the system, by adherence to a strict monetary rule whereby the rate of growth of the money supply is fixed at the appropriate rate, full employment growth without inflation will be realized.

The mainstream response

Like the monetarist response to inflation, the mainstream view goes along with the need to restrict aggregate demand until inflation rates are greatly reduced. This is a necessary condition for eliminating inflation. However, this response differs from the monetarist's in at least two important respects. First, proponents of this position are aware of the high unemployment costs of restrictive policies. For this reason they would be more prone to introduce policies to lessen the hardships of unemployment, e.g. maintain or expand welfare and unemployment benefits. Monetarists in contrast tend to favour a cutback in these programmes as a means of getting people back to work. Secondly, believers in the mainstream position are rather more sceptical of the ability of the economy to automatically right itself following a restrictive policy that succeeds in bringing down inflation rates. They would therefore caution the authorities that the design of the recovery programme is all important. In particular, it is necessary for the authorities to proceed with a recovery programme that does not lead corporations and unions to feel that the return to full employment will be permanent regardless of their behaviour. This is part of the credibility of policy. If this can be done, then there is no reason why full employment and price stability can not be maintained simultaneously without any drastic interference with the workings of collective bargaining and the price mechanism. Government intervention may be necessary from time to time but it will be of the conventional Keynesian type.

Post-Keynesian policy

The mainstream view today remains one in which means can be found for reflating the economy and returning to full employment without causing inflation rates to accelerate before this employment goal is attained. In this important sense this belief can be characterized as one that rejects the notion of an inherent tendency for inflation rates at full employment to accelerate. Advocates of the post-Keynesian position maintain that even if inflation rates can be reduced through restrictive policies, it will never be possible to so convince the public of their resolve that the authorities can ever count on a non-inflationary path back to full employment. The structural and institutional changes referred to earlier will never permit this scenario.

The policy alternatives to maintaining high rates of unemployment indefinitely if the post-Keynesian position is correct are fairly clear cut. If stimulative policies in and of themselves lead to accelerating rates of inflation under full or near full employment conditions, and if this policy is ruled out on political grounds, then the remaining alternative is a rather drastic policy response to current conditions.

The alternative to stagnation, on this view, is a permanent incomes policy. Since capitalism suffers from an inflationary bias whenever it achieves low rates of unemployment, full employment and price stability are only compatible if wage and price setting is somehow coordinated with the goals of price and wage stability. What form this incomes policy must take is still an open question. Most economists would be reluctant to propose statutory controls on wages and prices for more than a short period of time. Voluntary policies based on tripartite, consensus agreements or market incentives such as the tax-based incomes policy (TIP) are increasingly being offered today as alternative solutions.

THE IMPACT OF RESTRICTIVE POLICIES

The authors of this collection of papers fall into either the mainstream or post-Keynesian category. Unlike the monetarists, all would subscribe to the view that inflation is a mixture of demand-pull and cost-push elements. This is illustrated quite well in Lipsey's description of the causes of the acceleration of inflation rates in the late 1960s to early 1970s. Lundberg's detailed account of the breakdown of the 'Swedish model' is another example. All the writers would deny the automatic self-regulating properties of a modern capitalist system arguing instead for the need, in varying degrees, for government intervention. Godley's paper attempts to provide a framework for supporting this position. He sees the current debate over this issue as but the latest manifestation of a long-term dispute dating back a century and a half. Then as now Godley sees the need for active intervention in order to correct for potential malfunctions. And all would adhere to the position that institutional developments such as the rise of trade unions and oligopolies shape and influence not only the inflationary process but the policies that may be usefully introduced to combat inflation. This is very apparent in Sinclair's discussion of the impact of OPEC on the policy options available to the oil-importing countries.

What does come through in most of the papers and what importantly distinguishes them from monetarist writings is the recognition of the great costs involved in any 'victory over inflation', to use Tobin's expression. Restrictive aggregate demand policies do affect the real sector, i.e. output and employment, but not because of false perceptions or misinformation about the gains and losses of unemployment. They do so because most markets are fix-price and firms respond to slack demand by cutting back output and laying off workers, not by reducing prices to clear markets. Only later do restrictive policies begin to affect inflation, to a large extent by reducing wage demands and settlements in progressively looser labour markets.

Thus, the current widespread unemployment is recognized (sometimes only implicitly) by writers in this volume as largely involuntary, induced by policy makers in an effort to reduce inflation and also, in Sinclair's paper, to reduce payments deficits.

Additional costs of restrictive policies are mentioned by most of the writers. Lundberg, citing Verdoorn, attributes a good part of the recent productivity decline to the cutback in aggregate demand. Restrictive policies to fight inflation will create stagnation in this view.

Osberg's paper discusses why the authorities have been so willing to trade-off unemployment for price stability and incur such high costs. He concludes that bad economics has been an important and critical influence. Models of labour-market behaviour, appropriate under full employment conditions, were uncritically used to explain unemployment under conditions of widespread slack throughout the economy.

Tobin's, Lipsey's and Cornwall's papers discuss some of the reasons why the unemployment costs of restrictive policies have been so great relative to the results. Unlike the monetarists who think in terms of symmetries, these papers point up the likely existence of asymmetric responses of workers and firms to increases and decreases in demand and other influences that determine wages and prices. Inflation rates can be brought down, even though inflation may be partly or even largely a cost-push phenomenon, but it is harder to reduce rates of price and wage inflation by cutting back employment and sales than it is to

Introduction 15

accelerate them through stimulation. This may be due to forward-looking expectations but the importance of past events is given prominence in these essays. Stagflation can be explained partly in conventional Keynesian aggregate demand terms — reduced aggregate demand leads to increased unemployment and stagnation; and partly in terms of an extension of Keynes' downward rigidity of money wages — widespread wage and price rigidities keep inflation going in spite of slack conditions.

Lipsey cites the behaviour of the authorities as an additional critical factor, adding support to the credibility hypothesis. According to Lipsey, monetary policy 'worked' in the 1980s because it was applied very intensely. In contrast the 'gradualism' of the Bank of Canada's policies in the 1970s was ineffective because the financial and business communities found means to offset policy measures.

AFTER STAGFLATION

As Tobin points out the basic issue of macro policy is what happens if and when inflation is beaten and the authorities must decide whether to introduce stimulative aggregate demand policies in an effort to get back to full employment. Will inflation rates start to accelerate before anything like full employment is achieved? The notion of a non-accelerating inflation rate of unemployment (NAIRU) plays a prominent role in most of the papers and is very much tied in with the notion of an inflationary bias already cited.

For example, Osberg argues that one of the costs of the current unemployment is that workers will adopt defensive measures to protect their jobs in the event of any future restrictive policy. These measures act to reduce mobility and productivity growth which leads to stronger inflationary tendencies in labour markets whatever the rate of unemployment. In other words, the rate of unemployment at which inflation rates start to accelerate, the NAIRU rises. Naturally, the rate of inflation associated with low rates of involuntary unemployment will also rise.

The spectre of a high NAIRU or, more generally, a pronounced inflationary bias is a rising concern among economists and government officials today as inflation rates come down and attention turns to attacking the unemployment problem. In this respect Lundberg is the most optimistic of the authors of these papers. We learn from our past mistakes and means will be found for re-establishing a more prosperous state of affairs, even though he feels that we can never re-create the 'golden age' of capitalism of the 1950s and 1960s. Lipsey places a great emphasis on the need to carefully construct a recovery programme that minimizes the chances of inflation accelerating as the economy recovers. But in Lipsey's view the possibility that modern capitalist economies may have entered a period of accelerating rates of inflation cannot be ruled out. As a result it may be necessary for the monetary authorities to reaffirm their commitment to price stability by the use of restrictive policies. If true, the cost in terms of reduced growth of output and productivity, cited by Lundberg, must be recognized.

Tobin also advocates implementing policies now before recovery develops in earnest for reasons similar to Lipsey's. However, in his view, the concern among government officials that the NAIRU is now quite high may be so pervasive that the central bank of the United States may be unwilling to reduce unemployment rates much below double-digit figures. If true, then Lundberg's explanation of stagnation is again relevant. If unemployment rates are maintained permanently at, say, 8–10 per cent and rates of capacity utilization of the capital stock are similarly held down, then the rate of growth of demand, investment and productivity will be greatly retarded. This condemns the economy to one of perpetual stagnation without inflation and this remains true even if it is possible, in fact, to return to full employment without accelerating inflation. As long as central bankers think this is impossible and act on this belief, stagnation will follow stagflation.

WHAT IF THERE IS NO INFLATIONARY BIAS?

Even if it could be assumed that once inflation has been eliminated and the economy returned to pre-stagflation rates of unemployment, inflation rates would not accelerate again, Sinclair and Godley remind us that there are additional impediments to a return to full employment. In Sinclair's view, a country acting unilaterally may be in a position to handle a potential balance-of-payments constraint. If stimulative demand policies lead initially to a too rapid rise in imports, a vigorous exchange-rate policy can be used to correct this external imbalance. But any coordinated attempt to return to full employment by a wide number of countries is very likely to lead to a strong upward trend in the real price of oil.

Disregarding the impact of this on inflation (and rising prices in other international commodity markets that can be expected following a worldwide restimulation), there remains the unfavourable impact of an upward trend in real oil prices on the payments position of the oil-importing countries. Without energy conservation policies, agreements with OPEC or a reduction of OPEC's powers. Sinclair feels most oil-importing countries will be faced with a balance-of-payments constraint, i.e. large current deficits at full employment that cannot be reduced by (widespread) depreciation of currencies and cannot be covered on a long-term basis by borrowing. In the face of such a constraint, countries will be forced to reduce aggregate demand, even if no domestic inflationary pressures develop at full employment.

All of this suggests the need for further intervention by government in the form of an energy policy or an industrial policy that stimulates exports, and above all some kind of international cooperation in working out policies consistent with worldwide full employment, a matter taken up by Godley.

WHAT IF THERE IS AN INFLATIONARY BIAS?

Cornwall and Sinclair take the view that a permanent incomes policy will also be required if full employment is ever to be realized again, because of the existence of an inflationary bias. Any attempt to move to full employment through stimulative aggregate demand policies will lead to accelerating rates of inflation unless accompanied by some kind of incomes policy. On this view current restrictive policies are not a sufficient condition for permanently ending inflation *and* returning to full employment.

It should be noted that a workable incomes policy means that current restrictive policies are not even a necessary condition for eventually ridding the economy of accelerating inflation at full employment. Lundberg's paper describes the successful workings of a voluntary consensus incomes policy. The installation of the EFO model of wage guidelines during the 1950s and 1960s in Sweden permitted full employment to be realized at the same time as a rate of inflation consistent with international competitiveness. This was achieved through the coordination of collective bargaining with the macroeconomic goals of the government, through consensus between government, labour and employers, i.e. a consensus incomes policy.

Lundberg does not consider what conditions would be necessary for the successful re-introduction of this kind of incomes policy. Tobin briefly discusses an 'incentives' incomes policy (TIP), an alternative voluntary incomes policy in which compliance to wage and price guidelines is sought through a pre-announced set of financial rewards and penalties. But whatever kind of incomes policy is adopted, its success will largely depend upon the ability of governments to marshal widespread political support. This has an important implication. If full employment leads to accelerating inflation in the absence of an incomes policy and if the successful workings of such policies require mass political support, then Cornwall reminds us that 'inflation is always and everywhere a political phenomenon'.

CONCLUSION

The tone of the papers range from guarded optimism to pessimism in the ability of modern capitalist systems to return to 'normalcy', at least without drastic changes in political and economic institutions. None of the writers are content to let 'market forces' or 'invisible hands' have free play, nor do any of them advocate the replacement of 'humane capitalism' by some other form of economic system. In different ways the various papers stress a need for government to actively intervene if capitalism is to work properly again. The essays are written in as non-technical a manner as is consistent with the complexities of the issues. As a group the papers should be most helpful in the task of developing an alternative to economic decline. Certainly that was the intentions of the authors.

During the final stages of publication the authors were invited to add a brief 'postscript'. As the postscripts reveal, the papers are just as relevant today as ever and will be of value to policy makers for some time to come.

NOTES

1. Lest this seem an unfair treatment of the monetarist position the reader is encouraged to read chapters 11 and 23 of a recent textbook written by a monetarist. See M. Parkin, *Modern Macroeconomics*, Prentice-Hall Canada, Scarborough, Ontario, 1982. In the formal monetarist explanation of the

'natural rate hypothesis', institutions such as trade unions are completely ignored. Only voluntary, frictional unemployment is possible. Changes in employment are always the result of money illusion or 'price surprises' occurring in competitive markets that always clear. This kind of unrealistic framework is absolutely essential in deriving a short-run Phillips curve that disappears in the long-run.
2. A thorough account of the 'mainstream' view is found in *Towards Full Employment and Price Stability*, OECD, Paris, 1978.
3. The post-Keynesian view corresponds to what Tobin calls in his essay the 'pessimistic strand in the American neo-Keynesian' tradition as well as his description of the post-Keynesian position.

2

After Disinflation, Then What?

JAMES TOBIN

The 1970s will be the Age of Stagflation in the economic history books, and the 1980s are likely to be the Age of Disinflation. Today conquest of the stubborn inflation inherited from the previous decade is the dominant priority of economic policy throughout the democratic capitalist world. In Britain under Margaret Thatcher, in the United States under Federal Reserve Chairman Paul Volcker, and less dramatically in other advanced economies of Western Europe and Japan, relentlessly restrictive monetary and macro-economic policies are gradually grinding down world inflation rates.

These efforts, I believe, will eventually succeed. They are taking a longer time and exacting a greater toll than their protagonists expected or promised. But the patience of the public, even of the victims of the deep recession the policies produced, remains remarkably robust. So firmly entrenched is popular distaste for the inflation of the late 1970s that dramatic reversals of direction are unlikely even if the present leaders of the crusade are displaced.

The key to success in disinflation is bringing the pattern of wage increase down to the trend of growth in labour productivity. The weapon now in use is severe economic slack, unemployment of labour and excess industrial capacity, prolonged until businesses, workers, and trade unions give way on wages and prices in desperate and often vain attempts to save jobs and avert bankruptcies. It is no surprise that the strategy works. It will continue to work as long as large margins of slack persist, even if the 1981/82 recession comes to an end.

There is still considerable distance to go. Inflation rates are now in the upper single digits in the major advanced economies of North America, Western Europe, and Japan. The anti-inflation crusades aim at rates well below 5 per cent, if not actually zero.

After all, inflation control was a major concern of policy before OPEC shocks brought double-digit rates. In the United States, for example, 5 per cent inflation caused consternation both in the mid-1950s and in the Vietnam era. At the present and foreseeable pace, it seems, victory over inflation will take a couple more years at least, more if events in the Middle East inflict a third shock to oil supplies and prices.

Nevertheless I think it is not too soon to look forward to V-I (victory over inflation) Day, to think about what the economic landscape will look like, and to consider where we will go from there. Like any victorious war, this one will leave in its wake difficult problems and important issues of policy. We should start working on them now. Moreover, thoughtful consideration of the prospects after V-I Day relates to some current issues about how vigorously and by what weapons we prosecute the war.

THE ECONOMIC LANDSCAPE AFTER DISINFLATION

After two or more additional years of monetary disinflation, our economies will be badly wounded. Unemployment and excess capacity will still be high, compared to the norms of the 1950s, 1960s, and 1970s, even if modest recovery from the recession does occur. In the United States today, for example, 2 years of real growth of 4½ per cent per year, rates that forecasters would regard as extremely optimistic, would barely suffice to reduce unemployment from 10 to 8 per cent — a figure higher than that of business cycle troughs prior to 1975. Protracted high unemployment destroys human capital, especially among cohorts of youths and young adults who during their crucial formative years are denied the training and experience of holding jobs. Prolonged excess capacity likewise deters physical capital formation; business firms lack the actual and prospective profits that would induce them to make, and enable them to finance, new investments. Recession and stagnation also squeeze public-sector budgets; in the United States, the overhead capital — roads, streets, sewage systems, parks, schools — provided by state and local governments is not even being maintained and replaced, much less expanded to meet future requirements.

These are the irreversible and durable costs incident to the hundreds of billions of dollars of lost production during the war to subdue inflation. Our economies, stocked with less capital and less up-to-date technology, will be less productive even when and if prosperity restores more normal rates of utilization of labour and other resources.

These social costs are accompanied by symptoms of financial distress painful to thousands of business enterprises and millions of households. Personal and corporate bankruptcies are epidemic; nations too have to beg for 'restructuring' of their debts. In chain reactions, banks, other financial institutions, and other lenders are threatened too. In part these difficulties are intrinsic to disinflation. Those who borrowed long at interest rates they could cover only if their wages or profits or the values of their properties grew in dollar value at high rates of inflation are bound to be in trouble when inflation unexpectedly subsides. Fifteen per cent mortgages, with interest deductible from taxable income, were a bargain if the debtor's wages would rise at 10 per cent per year and the value of his house at 15 per cent per year; they are a heavy burden when wages are rising only 5 per cent and real estate prices are flat. The same is true of a company or municipality that expected to service high-interest bonds from sales or tax revenues regularly swollen by inflation.

The consequences are shifts of income and wealth, in the opposite direction from the gains to borrowers at the expense of lenders characteristic of unanticipated inflation. We are learning, or re-learning, that such shifts occur in both directions and cause serious social strains both ways. Economists are prone to say that these financial shocks are 'merely' redistributions; factories and houses and farms are still there even if their ownerships change and their fruits are differently divided. But the adjustments are often costly. Moreover, in the present difficulties more is involved than unexpected disinflation burdening borrowers who contracted to pay too high interest. Most debtors have also been hit by the real by-products of the disinflation. The unemployed car worker, Braniff and International Harvester, and Mexico all lost their markets. The resulting financial distress is symptomatic of the real social costs previously discussed, the immense sacrifices of real income due to the idleness of productive resources.

THE DUBIOUS PROSPECTS FOR FULL RECOVERY

I have suggested that when victory over inflation is achieved considerable slack will remain in the world's advanced capitalist economies. Unemployment will be high, excess capital capacity too, by comparison with previous years of prosperity. What will be the prospects of restoring more normal rates of utilization? To be concrete, suppose that in the United States inflation has been brought down 2 or 3 years from now to 2 or 3 per cent, while unemployment remains 8 per cent or higher. Could we then expect to reduce unemployment even as far as 6 per cent, where it stood in 1978/79? One could ask a similar question for Britain: when and if Mrs Thatcher's determined policy succeeds in getting inflation down, will unemployment then be brought down too?

Let me give some reasons for a pessimistic answer to those questions. V-I Day is a figure of speech, and a somewhat misleading one. No one, least of all the victorious generals, can be sure the war is over and won. There is no palpable enemy commander to yield his sword, disarm his troops, and sign a document of surrender. There are only price statistics and their changes over time. Maybe the next month, the next quarter, or the next year will bring bad news again. The anti-inflation crusaders will be very cautious. After all, they will say to themselves and to us, we have paid dearly for this victory; let us not throw it away now. We did that before, they will remind us, losing in subsequent expansions the gains against inflation won in 1957–60, 1970–1, and 1974–5. We must not rekindle inflationary psychology this time. Further recovery is bound to raise some sensitive commodity prices, and to encounter some bottlenecks in domestic and world supplies. Oil prices might shoot up again if prosperity expands world demand for energy too much and too fast, and one can never tell when there will be political disruptions of supply. Moreover, some important cost-based prices in our economies are still rising excessively, partly because they are still absorbing cost increases from the previous inflation – public utility rates and medical-care fees are prime examples.

Reasoning thus, these policy-makers will be content to let the economy resume a track of normal sustainable growth in production, i.e. one which keeps the margin of slack, as measured in unemployment and excess capacity, roughly constant. Real GNP would grow as much as the expansion of the labour force and the growth of productivity would permit, but not enough, even temporarily, to take up the residue of slack. Permanently higher unemployment, perhaps at least 8 per cent in North America, will be insurance against the resumption of inflation.

THE LEGACY OF MONETARISM

The likelihood of this scenario is reinforced by central banks' commitments to monetarist targets. Their strategy in the crusade for disinflation is gradually to reduce growth rates of monetary aggregates until they no more finance sustainable growth of real GNP at stable prices. In the United States, for example, the Federal Reserve has been cutting the year-to-year growth of transactions money, M-1, its principal target, since 1977, and has strongly emphasized its determination to follow this course since its well-publicized change in operating procedures in October 1979. The Reagan Administration, shortly after coming into power in 1981, endorsed the policy and asked that M-1 growth targets be cut in half by 1985, i.e. to around 2 per cent per year. The end of the process could be 0 per cent, because the upward trend in the velocity of transactions money, due to innovations in financial technology, might be sufficient to handle sustainable inflation-free growth of GNP, 2.5–3 per cent per year.

The monetarist view underlying policy in the United States and elsewhere, stresses the crucial role of expectations. Declining and ultimately stable money growth, with actual performance confirming announced intentions, is regarded as essential for cooling inflationary psychology and preventing its re-ignition. Achieving and maintaining 'credibility' is the watchword, and credibility is thought to be attached to monetary aggregates even more than to prices and nominal incomes. This is a strong additional reason why central banks will be reluctant to allow the burst of monetary growth, albeit temporary, needed to finance a slack-reducing economic recovery even when inflation has abated.

The transition from a monetarist strategy of disinflation to a monetarist recipe for stable growth involves another and somewhat more subtle difficulty. Successful disinflation will itself increase the demand for money, which will become a more attractive asset when its purchasing power is not depreciating. To put the point another way, nominal interest rates on substitute assets – time deposits, Treasury bills, commercial paper – will fall with disinflation, lowering the opportunity cost incentive for economizing holdings of transactions money, currency and checking account balances. Given an interest-elasticity of demand for M-1 estimated conservatively at 0.15 in absolute value, a nominal interest rate decline of 67 per cent as a result of disinflation would raise money demand by 10 per cent. The central bank would somehow have to accommodate this one-shot, non-recurrent, demand just to finance sustainable zero-inflation growth, quite apart from any period of exceptional real growth designed to diminish unemployment. But accommodation of extra money demand by temporarily higher money-growth targets — 5 per cent more in each of 2 years or 3 per cent more for 3 years — would endanger the central bank's hard-earned credibility.

The problem is even further exacerbated in the United States because legal ceilings on deposit interest rates are gradually being phased out. In a few years, we may expect, checkable deposits counted in M-1 will bear market-determined interest rates, differing from rates available on substitute assets only by costs of intermediation and transactions services. This reform too will augment the demand for M-1, as payment of controlled interest on checkable savings deposits ('NOW accounts') has already done, and as the popularity of checkable money-market funds, not included in M-1, indicates. The Federal Reserve recognizes that accommodating extra money demand from this source is innocuous, appropriate, even desirable, and has struggled to do so to date without exceeding its year-to-year targets. In future this may not be possible, so the credibility dilemma looms still again. Somehow the 'Fed' will have to persuade its constituencies that upward departures from its austere path of money growth are healthy, and do not signal retreat from its basic anti-inflationary stance.[1]

There is, to be sure, a way that extra monetary demand from any of the sources discussed, could in principle be satisfied without any departure, either in form or substance, from announced monetarist strategy and tactics. That is to prolong and extend the disinflationary transition to include a period of actual deflation. During that period the price level would have to fall enough to accommodate the extra demands for money. Some of you — especially any whose memory like mine includes the deflation of the 1930s — may find even the contemplation of such a scenario incredible. Remember, however, that in monetarist theory it is as easy for nominal wages and prices to fall as to rise, as easy to lower inflation from 1 per cent to −1 per cent as from 8 per cent to 6 per cent.

If this recital makes any of you feel that it is silly and dangerous for central banks to stake their credibility on targets for monetary aggregates whose velocity and meaning change both systematically and randomly, I would be pleased and not surprised. Elsewhere I have advanced other arguments to the same effect,[2] which I will not repeat here. Anyway the monetary authorities, at least the Federal Reserve, will some day have to extricate themselves from the monetarist trap they set for themselves. The best time is now, during the disinflationary transition.

THE UPWARD DRIFT OF THE 'NATURAL RATE' OF UNEMPLOYMENT

A basic issue of macroeconomic policy after V-I Day is what has happened to the 'natural rate of unemployment' or as it is sometimes more neutrally called the 'non-accelerating inflation rate of unemployment' (NAIRU). If it is 4, 5 or 6 per cent, then policy-makers should not be content with steady sustainable growth while unemployment is stuck at 8 per cent. But maybe they believe that the NAIRU is now 8 per cent, that no smaller unemployment rate is compatible with stable prices or with any stable, non-increasing, rate of inflation. No one can be sure. Policy-makers might, for example, estimate the expected value of the NAIRU to be 6 per cent but assign some probability to lower and higher values. They might then aim at 8 per cent because they consider the costs of inflation resulting from going lower than the NAIRU to exceed the costs of running the economy chronically with 'unnaturally' high unemployment.

How low an unemployment rate can the economy, with the help of macroeconomic policy, achieve and sustain? Over the past 30 years views of economists and policy-makers have become more pessimistic, almost monotonically. In 1952/53, after the Korean war build-up and inflation, prices stabilized with unemployment as low as 3 per cent. In the mid-1950s, however, inflation of 4 per cent plus seemed to be heating up with unemployment at 4 per cent plus, inspiring monetary and fiscal policies that led to two recessions in rapid succession and lowered inflation to the 1–2 per cent range. The official unemployment target of the Kennedy–Johnson administration was 4 per cent, and it was reached with negligible inflation cost in 1965. President Johnson's decision, against his economists' advice, to spend for his Vietnam adventure without raising taxes led to an excess-demand inflation, lowering unemployment as far as 3 per cent while raising inflation to 5 per cent. After the anti-inflation recession of 1969–71 yielded disappointing results, President Nixon imposed wage and price controls and macroeconomic policies turned expansionary. This time the boom was deliberately ended by restrictive policy with 5 per cent unemployment, and with inflation accelerating in frightening degree, led by international commodity markets and by OPEC oil prices. The next United States recovery, from 1975 to 1979, was deliberately cut off with unemployment around 6 per cent, again as a result of an alarming surge of inflation, featuring the second OPEC shock.

What accounts for the apparent high level of 'natural' unemployment and for its secular increase? If measured unemployment is not Keynesian involuntary unemployment, capable of being reduced by demand expansion without unleashing pressure for higher real wages, what is it? The other adjectives are frictional, search, voluntary, and classical; they are not exclusive, one of the others.

Frictional unemployment is matched by job vacancies. Data on vacancies comparable to those for unemployment are not available for the United States, but two conclusions would be generally accepted. One is that meaningful vacancies in aggregate do not begin to match the number of unemployed even in prosperous times. The other is that in America, as in countries where vacancies data exist, the vacancy rate has risen secularly relative to the unemployment rate. This is indicated in the United States by the trend of the index of help-wanted advertising.

Frictional unemployment may represent active voluntary search between jobs by unemployed workers, especially youth and young adults. In the 1960s and 1970s the demographic composition of the labour force shifted in this direction, though now it is moving the other way. Voluntary unemployment, whether for selective search or not, is fostered by unemployment insurance and by other transfer benefits available to the unemployed. As these benefits have become more generous – partly indeed in response to higher unemployment rates – they may well have dulled incentives to stay employed and to seek and accept new jobs.

'Classical' unemployment may be due to restraints of trade that fix real wages too high, union monopolies or minimum-wage legislation. These restraints can make individual workers involuntarily unemployed, but the remedy is more effective competition in labour markets rather than demand stimulus.

THE UNEMPLOYMENT–INFLATION TRADEOFF: ALTERNATIVE DIAGNOSES

From this history several different lessons could be drawn, with radically conflicting policy implications. The orthodox conclusion, the accepted diagnosis supporting current policy, is that the NAIRU has been chronically and over-optimistically overestimated, so that policy has consistently erred on the inflationary side. The NAIRU has been steadily increasing, so that attempts to restore the unemployment rates of previous prosperities have blown up in inflation. Maybe unemployment is too high, but that is a problem for microeconomic structural policy, not for macroeconomic demand management.

A variant of this position, a modern version of classical economic doctrine, is that a market economy will find equilibrium on its own, in unemployment as in other variables. Whatever unemployment the economy settles into, under stable policies like monetarist rules described above, will be the equilibrium, natural and non-accelerating inflation rate. Economists and policy-makers cannot know what it is numerically and should not aim at any particular value of unemployment or of any other real economic variable. These diagnoses and prescriptions are pessimistic about unemployment, placing it beyond the reach of macroeconomic demand management by monetary and fiscal measures.

An alternative reading of recent history, for want of a better word let us call it a neo-Keynesian analysis, is in one sense more optimistic and in another more pessimistic. The stagflation of the 1970s and especially the double-digit inflations at the peaks of the two prosperities were not endemic. They were the results of supply and price shocks of unprecedented severity. History, from the Vietnam escalation in 1966 through the Iranian revolution, has bequeathed us a high inflation rate; monetary efforts to contain and conquer inflation have brought high unemployment rates. Though the inflation is accidental in origin and arbitrary in magnitude, it has become embedded in habits, patterns, and expectations and has acquired a stubborn momentum of its own. That is why disinflation is so time-consuming and so costly in employment and production.

But once the process is completed and new lower patterns of wage and price increase are established, they too will tend to persist in the absence of a new sequence of extraordinary shocks like those of the last 16 years. Restore the initial conditions of 1961 and we can enjoy the prosperous and non-inflationary expansion of 1961–5. Maybe the NAIRU is now a point or more higher than 4 per cent, though that cannot be proved by the experience of 1973 or 1979. In some measure the NAIRU follows actually experienced unemployment. Thus the high unemployment of the 1970s, by destroying human capital and by deterring investment and lowering excess capital capacity relative to human unemployment, has temporarily raised the NAIRU. By the same token, prudent expansionary policies will lower both actual unemployment and the 'natural rate'.

At the same time, there is a more pessimistic strand in this American neo-Keynesian tradition. Long before the stagflation of the 1970s, indeed as early as the 1940s, its adherents detected an inflationary bias in the wage- and price-setting institutions of modern capitalism. Wages and mark-ups are, they perceived, more responsive upward to demand stimuli than downward to demand reductions. As a result, inter-industry and inter-regional shifts in demand and business activity tend to be inflationary in aggregate, and likewise cyclical fluctuations generate a higher inflationary trend than stable growth. It is difficult to combine price stability and full employment in the sense of 'natural' labour market equilibrium. The NAIRU is not full employment in any equilibrium or welfare sense; some margin of involuntary unemployment is necessary to contain inflation. The bias was especially severe in the face of the supply and price shocks of the 1970s; it took an inordinate amount of slack to make non-energy costs and prices compensate for the large increases in oil prices.

This view of the world has led some of its exponents to advocate incomes policies. In the placid early 1960s, informal wage–price guideposts were invoked to keep the expansion free of inflation and, one might say, to make the NAIRU coincide with full employment. Recently neo-Keynesians have advocated incomes policies, for example tax rewards or penalties to induce compliance with guideposts, in order to speed disinflation and limit its damage to employment and production. Conceivably incomes policies could be used, as in 1961–5, as insurance against resumption of inflation during recovery from the current disinflationary slump, substituting for the insurance provided by maintaining a permanently large margin of slack.

A third view, sometimes called post-Keynesian, is more pessimistic about the wage- and price-setting mechanisms of modern capitalism. These mechanisms, far from being competitive markets, reflect conflicts among groups with significant economic and political power. Their effective claims on the national product add to more than the total product, and there are no natural market processes capable of resolving this fundamental disharmony. Of this unreconciled conflict, inflation is one symptom. But macroeconomic restriction by monetary and fiscal policy cannot overcome either the struggle or its inflationary symptoms. It can only shrink the size of the pie, and that will not make the claimed shares add up, or rather add down. From this standpoint, the substantial content of Mrs Thatcher's policies in Britain, and to a much lesser degree of President Reagan's, is to destroy the power of trade unions, relative to those of other players. In America the characteristic post-Keynesian recommendation is the imposition of permanent price and wage controls on major corporations and unions, as long advocated by J. K. Galbraith.

POLICIES TO IMPROVE THE TRADEOFF

As divergent as these viewpoints are, they concur on one point: V-I Day will merit only one or two cheers. Of stagflation the 'inflation' will be subdued, but the 'stag' will remain. Reconciliation of a tolerably stable trend in the value of money with satisfactory performance in employment and production will be, as before, a terribly challenging task. Moreover, it may well be beyond the capacity of the conventional fiscal and monetary tools of macroeconomic management by themselves. Auxiliary measures are likely to be necessary, at least prudent. Even monetarists and born-again classical economists, who are complacently confident of the ability of competitive markets to find equilibrium employment and production, would generally agree to microeconomic reforms to improve the efficiency of markets and in the process to diminish unemployment. Economists of other schools have other auxiliary policies and reforms in mind.

I propose now to review the major proposals. At one extreme are structural reforms designed to make markets more competitive, more consonant with the classical model. At the other extreme are permanent wage and price controls, whose advocates take concentrations of economic power as ineradicable features of modern capitalism. In between are pragmatic suggestions that defy doctrinal or ideological categorization. In discussing this spectrum my stress will be on the great macroeconomic dilemma, unemployment and inflation, not on the entire range of issues involved in various proposals. That is why the discussion will focus principally on labour markets and wage determination.

CENTRALIZED AND SYNCHRONIZED COLLECTIVE BARGAINING?

Wage-setting institutions and the behaviour of employers, workers, and unions determine the position of the NAIRU and the responses of money wage rates to expansions and contractions of monetary demand and to price movements. Are there structural and institutional changes which would ameliorate the trade-offs between unemployment and inflation? In North America nominal wages respond more slowly both to unemployment and to price movement than in most European economies. Could we, should we, make them more responsive? Some of our problems apparently arise from asymmetries in short-run response; wages, prices, and their rates of change move up more readily than they move down. Could we engineer greater symmetry, or even reverse the asymmetry? Do our institutions of collective bargaining, which also differ from those of other economies, make macroeconomic stabilization more difficult?

In the United States and Canada wage-setting is decentralized; there is no national bargain, not even an advisory guide agreed by national employers' and trade unions' federations after consultation with government. The advantage of a centralized bargaining institution is that the parties can understand the macroeconomic situation of the country, the monetary and fiscal policies of the government, and the consequences of greater and lesser wage settlements. The consultations can be a two-way street, in which the parties also influence macro policies. Remote economy-wide considerations are not prime considerations in decentralized local bargains. Economy-wide bargaining cannot work and may yield dangerously explosive results if there is an irreconcilable conflict of power and interest between the parties. Nor can it work if the bargaining federations lack or lose influence over their constituents. In the United States national organizations with the requisite legitimacy do not exist. Neither does the community of interest in international competitiveness that has facilitated agreement in smaller and more open economies. Wage-setting in North America will remain decentralized, with any national 'guideposts' to which leaders of industry and labour lend moral support depending on government initiatives, i.e. incomes policies.

Wage-setting in our economies is not only decentralized but also unsynchronized. Collective bargaining contracts vary in duration from 1 to 3 years, with irregularly staggered dates of renegotiation. Employer-administered wage scales are generally adjusted annually, but at diverse times of year. A centralized system is necessarily more synchronized, with uniformly annual contract reopenings and wage-settings concentrated in one season of the year. The American system, it is widely agreed, contributes to the sluggishness of nominal wages and prices in the face of fluctuations in economic activity and unemployment. Multi-year contracts work in this direction. Staggered wage-setting does too, by accentuating emulative patterns of behaviour designed to maintain relative wages – catching up with or leap-frogging over settlements in other industries and unions.

Some observers, therefore, suggest legislation to impose greater synchronization on our decentralized system, forbidding contracts longer than 1 year, perhaps even prescribing uniform dates. The idea is to make wages respond more promptly to current realities of the economy and labour markets. Like most recommendations on this subject, this one is double-edged. Less sluggish, more responsive, nominal wages would clearly be macroeconomically advantageous in periods like the present. Recession would do its anti-inflationary job more quickly and with less contraction of employment and production. But cyclical upswings might generate more inflation, and sooner. Moreover, the sluggishness of nominal wages in America, in contrast to most European countries, facilitated the adjustment of real wages to the oil price shocks of the 1970s. This was accomplished in true Keynesian fashion, as the money-wage trend fell behind cost-of-living inflation even while employment and activity were rising. In Europe there was greater rigidity of *real* wages, a major reason why recovery there after 1974 was weaker and slower.

There are, of course, microeconomic objections to the synchronization proposal, a major intervention into 'free' collective bargaining and even into employer-administered wage-setting. Multi-year contracts were adopted to give both sides more security against work stoppages, more certainty in future planning, and more relief from the costs of negotiation. I should interject that I think objections of this kind should be judged pragmatically, not accepted as matters of principle. Unions and collective bargaining are protected and governed by the state, by a complicated code of rights and procedures; correspondingly the state has the right to regulate in the public interest the process and the contracts that result.

INDEXATION

Indexation is a related but separable issue. It too is double-edged. When macroeconomic policies and events are bringing disinflation, when flexible commodity prices are weakening and even falling, when exchange-rate appreciation is lowering the domestic prices of internationally traded goods, wage indexing speeds the process of disinflation and limits its damaging real consequences. In the opposite circumstances, it accelerates inflation and restricts real economic expansion. In 1974 and after, full indexation common in Europe was another obstacle to adjustment to the oil shock, while the incompleteness of wage indexing in America facilitated the real-wage adjustment previously mentioned.

Asymmetric indexation, for example uncapped up but limited on the down side, yields the worst of both worlds. Even when agreements on base wages are frequently reopened, the spirit of indexation can introduce perverse asymmetry, rendering unthinkable any downward adjustment of real wages. Given the asymmetries, a case could be made for forbidding wage indexation in collective-bargaining contracts. Short of that extreme, government could withhold its sanction and enforcement from non-symmetrical indexing provisions of contracts. In any case, the government should construct and publish, recommend, perhaps even require a suitable price index. One thing we learned in the 1970s is that the customary Consumer Price Index is not suitable. It includes items – notably adverse shifts in terms of external trade and indirect taxes – against whose increase neither government nor employers can be expected to insure workers or other citizens. Some countries, Austria and Sweden to my knowledge, have purged the index used in wage agreements and transfer payments of such items. In the United States short-term movements of the CPI were also distorted by faulty technical procedures that exaggerated the effects of increases in nominal interest rates on home mortgages and in residential real-estate prices.

GAIN-SHARING?

Japan these days is the envied model economy, and Western observers naturally wonder whether we could emulate institutions of labour relations that apparently combine low unemployment and low inflation. Flexibility of wage costs in Japanese industry is obtained by making a significant fraction of labour compensation contingent on the firm's sales and earnings, paid as annual bonuses rather than as contracted or pre-set wages. Daniel Mitchell of UCLA proposes a similar system – he calls it 'gain-sharing' – for the United States, though the contingent compensation would be spelled out in formulae in advance, rather than left to employers' discretion.[3] The recommendation is addressed more to unions and managements than to legislators, although presumably some tax incentives could be offered as encouragement, at least initially. The US tax code already encourages profit-sharing, but it has never been popular with either management (except for managers) or organized labour. The bonus system fits better the all-encompassing paternalism and the lifetime employment commitments in Japan than the strictly business-like spirit of American labour–management relations. But we shall see. *In extremis*, where many American firms and workers find themselves as a result of Japanese competition, Mitchell's proposal may appear quite attractive.

TRADE-UNION POWER

Reforms congenial to many economists would diminish or break the bargaining power of trade unions, which they view as monopolies restraining trade with government support. But many of the same economists have also denied that labour monopolies, any more than product monopolies, have significant *macro*economic consequences. I suspect that they do, if only because administered and negotiated wages and prices contribute to the stickiness and sluggishness of wage and price adjustment discussed above. It is true, however, that in the United States these phenomena antedated both widespread labour organization and the legislation encouraging and protecting it.

Another channel by which union power has macroeconomic effects could be by increasing the NAIRU, as follows. When unions impose higher than market-clearing wages in organized industries, workers are thrown into competitive sectors, lowering market-clearing real wages there. But minimum wages in force by legislation or custom may prevent their employment. Or the lower wage available to them may make unemployment more attractive while waiting and seeking for a high-wage job, especially for those eligible for unemployment compensation.

Unions have sometimes been accused of initiating 'cost-push' inflation, though it seems irrational for them to postpone for a 'push' the exploitation of any monopoly power they possess. The world-wide wage explosion of 1970–1 seemed like wage-push, because it was hard to explain by previous wage or price inflation or by contemporaneous tightness of labour markets. Possibly the struggle for relative wage positions, to which union rivalries contribute, becomes on occasion dynamically unstable — at least that happened in those years among construction trades in the United States. The unusual gains of union wages relative to non-union wages in the later 1970s in the United States may indicate another push.

Finally, in a wholly syndicalized society, collective union power claiming the lion's share of national product is a macroeconomic problem far exceeding in gravity its inflationary symptoms. I do not place Canada and the United States in this category of hopelessly conflicted societies.

In our countries, I think, the problem is that the unemployed, especially the never-employed and the non-union, have precious little voice in the determination of wages, in the local and national trade-offs of wages and jobs. The insiders, the employed, and among them the senior workers, control union policies; indeed they have the greatest influence on employers in unorganized shops as well. Workers at the factory gate, willing to replace those inside at lower wages, have little direct effect on wages. Recession and depression generate unemployment, but their main effect on wages comes via the financial and market pressures that impair employers' ability to pay and stiffen their backbones. Big wage concessions come, as we have observed recently in the automotive industry, when employers facing bankruptcy can credibly threaten senior workers with losses of jobs and pensions, via wholesale permanent closings. Cheap labour eventually disciplines the wages of established workers through competition from new products, new technologies, new firms, new regions, and foreign countries. Our economy would function better, both micro-economically, if the discipline of wages by unemployed workers were exerted more directly and more quickly.

Writing about these issues 16 years ago, I observed

> that the bargaining powers of unions are in considerable degree granted to them by federal legislation. In return for these privileges, it seems to me, the public could require unions to be effectively open to new members and apprentices. It is especially important to eliminate racially discriminatory barriers to entry.[4]

This still seems reasonable, indeed minimal. Certainly the federal government should not reinforce and extend union power by measures that require union scale wages to be paid on projects directly or indirectly, wholly or partially, federally financed, even to non-union workers in locations where no union scale is otherwise effective. The infamous Davis-Bacon Act has been on the hit list of every Council of Economic Advisers and Budget Office in living memory.

MINIMUM WAGES AND UNEMPLOYMENT INSURANCE

Minimum wage legislation probably does make the NAIRU higher, especially increasing youth unemployment. But the evidence is that its effects are greatly exaggerated in conservative rhetoric. United States law allows many exceptions and exemptions. Since the minimum wage did not rise in real terms or relative to median wages in the 1970s, it can hardly be blamed for the increase in unemployment. Similar remarks apply to unemployment compensation. No doubt it increases the NAIRU, the more so the more liberal the standards of eligibility, the duration of benefits, and their size relative to prevailing wages. Quantitatively the effects are small relative to observed unemployment; moreover, liberalizations during the 1970s, many of them in response to high unemployment in the recession of 1974/75, cannot account for more than a few tenths of a point of unemployment. Recently unemployment compensation was made taxable as income for taxpayers with incomes inclusive of this compensation exceeding $20000. Further reforms would be possible without impairing the 'safety net' the system provides. They would include tightening the connection between an employer's contribution rate and the claims attributable to layoffs by the employer. At present employers and employees, especially in seasonal businesses, can collude tacitly or otherwise and shift to other taxpayers part of the employees' annual wage.

MANPOWER POLICIES

I referred above to the rise in frictional unemployment indicated by the rise in vacancies relative to unemployment. Measures which make unemployment and prolonged search less attractive would reduce this contribution to the NAIRU. So should a host of labour-market policies, some of which have been tried for at least two decades with little evident effect. These include improving the exchange of information about jobs and available workers; training and retraining on and off the job; assistance in relocation. Martin Baily and I have shown how government programmes to create jobs for low-wage and unskilled workers, either by direct employment or by subsidies, could 'cheat' the Phillips curve in the short run and lower the NAIRU in the long run.[5]

OTHER STRUCTURAL REFORMS

I have spoken too long about labour markets and unions. There are other targets of structural reform. Government support of agricultural prices imparts another perverse asymmetry to the macroeconomy; the prices go up without impediment when demand—supply conditions are favourable, but supports hinder their fall when the dice roll the other way. Businesses raise prices when their sales, production, and employment are declining; the anti-trust lawyers in the Department of Justice should take notice. In Washington, Ottawa, and other capitals knowledgeable economists have well-known lists of 'sacred cows', inflation-increasing and efficiency-reducing laws and regulations with unassailable political support. Unfortunately one consequence of economic distress of the present virulence is that more and more claims for protection against competition, foreign and domestic, become irresistible in Congress or Parliament.

INCOMES POLICIES

It is easier to enumerate possible structural reforms than it is to muster confidence that much will actually be done or that they would greatly change the situation. That is why discussions of this kind always come in the end to incomes policies. These range from Kennedy–Johnson guideposts – open-mouth policy, without teeth – to full-fledged Nixonian or Galbraithian controls. They include economists' favourites, Abba Lerner's negotiable ration vouchers legally required of firms raising their average wages, and Tax-based Incomes Policies (TIP) advocated by such diverse authors as Weintraub, Wallich and Okun, which induce compliance with guideposts by rewards or penalties.[6] Those are my favourites too. I would embellish usual TIP proposals, if possible, by special penalties for increases of wages or mark-ups by firms whose employment and production are declining.

As in 1961, it is important to pave the way for a non-inflationary recovery from years of stagnation. Nervousness about resumption of inflation is more acute now, both among private agents and among policy-makers, than 20 years ago. Consequently guideposts need more teeth, such as TIP could provide, than the Kennedy guideposts had then. They also need the understanding and support of leaders of business and labour. The promise of genuine and full recovery, promoted by monetary and fiscal policy, would be a strong inducement, a welcome change from vaguely threatening indifference to private-sector wage and price behaviour. Without strong leadership from Presidents and Prime Ministers, the climate of opinion necessary for successful incomes policies cannot be created or maintained.

Incomes policies have a bad reputation because they are difficult to administer and because they inevitably distort market allocations of resources. TIP is designed to minimize these inefficiencies and to allow flexibility. When market signals are strong, firms can exceed guideposts, foregoing some rewards for themselves and their employees or incurring some penalties. These costs can be justified by the externalities incident to the value the society places on the avoidance of inflation. The economy-wide costs of incomes policy must be weighed against the social costs of avoiding inflation by macroeconomic policies that run the economy at chronically low speed. Those, in my view, are orders of magnitude greater. Let me emphasize also that it is not proposed to use incomes policies to contain and suppress excess demand inflation; we know from experience that you can not keep the lid on a boiling pot. The purpose rather is to guard against the revival of an inflationary dynamic, arising from the structural biases of the economy or from cost-pushes or from expectations, even while the economy is operating within the bounds of full employment and normal capacity utilization.

My fear is that the purely monetary strategy of disinflation now, and inflation control thereafter, condemns our economies to chronic excess unemployment and to permanent weakness. Indeed I would not wait for V-I Day to engineer a recovery, preferably assisted by incomes policies to assure continued disinflation. Since the Second World War our pragmatic amalgam of capitalism and democracy in North America, Western Europe, and Japan spectacularly refuted the indictments and prophecies of Marx and other opponents. It would be ironic, maybe fatal, if we were now to concede by thought and deed that our system cannot function without an industrial reserve army of unemployed.

POSTSCRIPT

In the fourteen months since I wrote this Killam lecture, the main macro-economic event has been the upswing of economic activity in North America. The United States recession reached bottom in November–December 1982; production and employment recovered briskly throughout 1983. The turnabout was due to a deliberate change in Federal Reserve policy in the late summer and fall of 1982. Alarmed by the severe economic decline in America and elsewhere, by the possibility of a further collapse more difficult to reverse, by threatened financial insolvencies at home and abroad, Federal Reserve Chairman Volcker and his colleagues relented. It was not quite V-I Day, but the rate of inflation of the comprehensive 'GNP deflator' price index was below 4 per cent per year, six points below the years 1979 and 1980. The 1983 recovery was fueled not only by interest rate reductions following the easing of monetary policy but also by fiscal stimuli from tax cuts effective in July 1982 and July 1983 and from defense procurement. By ironic accident, budget policies adopted in 1981 motivated by 'supply-side' economics and national security considerations, turned out to be well-timed counter-cyclical demand management.

The Federal Reserve is, however, very nervous about the pace of recovery and the possibility of new inflationary consequences. Real interest rates are still very high, and the Federal Reserve is clearly prepared to slow or stop the recovery, even at unemployment rates one to three points higher than those achieved in the two recoveries of the 1970s, whenever wages and prices seem to be accelerating. Moreover, Europe and Japan have not shared in the 1983 recovery. The governments of those countries have not adopted actively expansionary monetary policies, and their fiscal policies are actively restrictive. Unemployment and other indicators of economic slack are still rising throughout most of the advanced economies of the free world. Incomes policies are still anathema. The dismal prospect described in the text — stagnation due to the risk of inflation and the absence of any other means of insuring against it — is still all too probable.

NOTES

1. Beginning in late summer of 1982, the Federal Reserve did suspend its targets for monetary aggregates, particularly M-1, for the reasons given above. In July 1983 the 'Fed' announced new targets for 1983 and 1984 monetary growth, de-emphasizing M-1 and re-basing its M-1 targets to make clear that no effort would be made to eliminate the above-target bulge of M-1 during the previous two quarters. Financial markets took these pragmatic moves in their stride.
2. Tobin, J. (1980) Stabilization policy ten years after, *Brookings Papers on Economic Activity*, **1**, 50–2; (1983) Financial structure and monetary rules, *Kredit und Kapital*, **16**, 2, 155–71; (1983) Monetary policy in an uncertain world, *Bank of Japan Monetary and Economic Studies*, **1**, 2, 15–28; (1983) Monetary policy: Rules, targets, and shocks, *Journal of Money, Credit, and Banking*, xv, 4, 506–18.
3. Mitchell, D. J. B. (1982) Gain sharing: An anti-inflation reform, *Challenge*, **25**, 3, 18–25.
4. Tobin, J. (1967) Unemployment and inflation: The cruel dilemma. In Almarin Phillips, ed., *Price Issues in Theory, Practice, and Policy*, Philadelphia: University of Pennsylvania Press, pp. 101–7. Reprinted, 1975, as Chapter 25 in my *Essays in Economics*, **2**, Amsterdam: North-Holland Pub. Co., pp. 3–10.
5. Baily, M. and Tobin, J. (1977) Macroeconomic effects of selective public employment and wage subsidies, *Brookings Papers on Economic Activity*, **2**, 511–41.
6. For a general survey and criticism of these proposals, see Okun, A. M. and Perry, G. L. (eds) (1978) *Curing Chronic Inflation*, Washington: Brookings Institution.

3

After Monetarism

RICHARD G. LIPSEY

The world is in the midst of, and possibly just beginning its recovery from, a policy-induced recession. Sponsored by the Federal Reserve System and aided, and abetted by the Bank of Canada and the British government, a policy of tight money and high interest rates has plunged the world's economies into the deepest recession since the Great Depression of the 1930s.

In this paper I briefly observe how we got into our present situation. I then discuss the current situation and ask what lessons we can learn from it. Finally I consider how a future policy for a low inflation rate might be structured.

I do not raise the vexing question of whether or not it is worth paying a heavy price to control inflation. I will merely make three observations on that issue.

First, economists have yet to reach any consensus on the costs of inflation. Their opinions range from the view that the costs are trivial, to the view that the costs are enormous and include an erroding of the entire social fabric.

Secondly, there is one alleged reason for *eliminating* inflation that should be noticed since it appears to provide a *sufficient* reason for needing to do so. It is sometimes argued that if we accept x per cent inflation, where x is any positive number, the inflation rate will accelerate until soon we have $2x$, then $3x$, and so on. According to the inflation models of both monetarists and Keynesians inflation tends to be stable if, and only if, unemployment is at its 'natural rate'. This stable rate can be any value. It follows that it is just as easy, or hard, to stabilize a zero inflation rate as it is to stabilize some positive rate by adopting policies to hold national income at its potential level and unemployment at its natural rate (by natural forces or policy interventions).

If 10 per cent cannot be stabilized because of, say, the effects of fluctuations around the natural rate, then neither can 0 per cent.

Thirdly, the fact that the general public, and the politicians who respond to their views, regard inflation as a serious problem is sufficient to make it a serious problem. Policies for controlling inflation will be imposed whether or not economists agree with the objective. So economists have a responsibility to try to make anti-inflation policies as high yielding as possible in terms of controlling inflation and as low cost as possible in terms of undesirable side effects. It is from this point of view that I approach the inflation issue here.

HOW DID WE GET WHERE WE ARE?

There is some debate about the causes of the rising inflation rates in the decade that preceded the opening of the anti-inflationary campaigns in the mid 1970s. Monetarists blame it all on monetary policy (see for example, Parkin, 1982); structuralists blame it all on supply-side effects (see for example, Barber and McCallum, 1980); Keynesians accept monetary factors but add inertias and supply-side shocks (see for example, Tobin 1980). This latter view gives monetary laxness a prime place but adds two further factors. First, what may be called the fundamental Keynesian asymmetry: prices rise quickly in periods of excess demand but fall only slowly in periods of excess supply. Second, supply-side shocks, which may have included the European wage explosion in 1968/69, and certainly included agricultural- and oil-price shocks in 1973/74, gave an added upward push to inflation rates. This majority view is expounded for example by Alan Blinder (1979) in his book on the Great Stagflation.

When the boom of the early 1970s ended in 1973, the OECD countries were averaging two-digit inflation. It was an inflation that had become firmly entrenched both in expectations and in institutional changes that reflected the new view that long-term contracts made in nominal money terms had acquired a large added risk component because of uncertainties about the inflation rate (with outcomes in the high range, appearing very much more probable than they had in the 1950s and 1960s).

Supply-side shocks coming from food, basic materials and energy prices helped to convert the recession into a stagflation.

This disaster finally persuaded the public and governments that inflation was a serious problem. The Federal Reserve adopted a tight monetary policy that, in 1974/75, forced the American economy through a sharp recession that was accompanied by a halving of the inflation rate. In Canada, a tough anti-inflationary monetary and fiscal policy was avoided on the grounds that the costs in terms of unemployment and lost output would be too high (see Government of Canada, 1975). Instead, wage and price controls were used in an attempt to force inflation down slowly in line with a gradual reduction in the rate of monetary growth. The food component of prices introduced quite a bit of short-term noise into the Consumer Price Index (CPI), but the CPI, excluding food, showed a steady decline during the 3 years of the controls programme as did negotiated wage settlements.

By the end of 1975 the recession was over and Canada was left with an inflation rate (December 1975 to December 1976) of 9.5 per cent which compared unfavourably with the United States rate of 7.0 per cent. The American inflation rate, however, crept up steadily during the long, slow recovery during the last half of the decade, and by 1980 had once again reached two-digit figures.

The Bank of Canada officially embraced monetarism in late 1975. It then adopted the policy of holding the rate of monetary growth within a target range, the range itself being gradually reduced. By and large the Bank was remarkably successful in meeting its targets. The underlying Canadian inflation rate did come down from 1975 to 1978 but then it turned around and soon was back in the two-digit range. Although the acceleration coincided with the end of the wage–price controls, econometric research does not suggest that this was a post-controls bubble, but rather the response of prices to the recovery. The resurgence of inflation in the face of a gradual reduction in the rate of growth of M1 meant a substantial rise in the income velocity of circulation of M1. Having been almost trend free at a value of 11 per cent of national income in the early part of the decade, M1 balances fell steadily starting in 1974, and reached a value of only 7.5 per cent of income in 1981 (in other words, M1 velocity rose from 9 to 13.3).

A lively debate broke out at the end of the decade as to whether Canadian policy of monetary gradualism had failed (see for example, *Canadian Public Policy*, Supplement 7, 239–48). With the hindsight of several years, it seems to me that the answers to the issues then debated are fairly clear. First, the policy of gradualism did fail in the sense that its main objective of moderating the rate of inflation was not achieved. Secondly gradualism failed because of some identifiable policy mistakes. Thirdly the failure of gradualism did not discredit monetary policy in general. Let us consider each of these points in a little more detail.

The first point is obvious. The inflation rate of 1980 of 10.1 per cent was not significantly below the 1975 rate of 10.8 per cent (and it was rising).

Secondly, the failure of gradualism was partly due to a mistaken reaction to major shifts in the demand for money that occurred in 1978/79 and 1981. It is easy to see with the benefit of hindsight that the Bank should have revised its money-supply targets downwards when the money-demand function shifted downwards. But it did not (and that is an illustration of why monetary policy must always remain an art rather than a blind, rule-following exercise) so the desired monetary stringency never occurred because (real) demand for money fell along with its supply. Furthermore, the Bank should have noticed the changing relation between its chosen target M1 and its policy objective, money national income. The velocity figures for M1 already quoted, and for M2, should have provided a warning. The income velocity of M2 was utterly stable until the mid 1970s when it began a gradual decline. It would appear, therefore, that there was a major substitution from M1 balances that are included in M2 but not in M1. The failure of gradualism was not unlike the failure of the fiscal policy experiment of 1968/69 in the United States. The main message is that there is a lot of random noise in the system. If the policy change is within say one standard deviation of the mean value of the noise, there is a good chance that its effects will not be noticeable. To be fully sure of being noticed, changes will have to be large in relation to the normal noise in the system. Shifts in the demand functions for monetary assets were major producers of monetary noise over the period.

Thirdly, many people felt that the basic relations assumed in monetary theory were wrong and that the failure of gradualism proved this. There is no reason to accept that gradualism's failure was monetarism's failure since gradualism hardly changed the monetary parameters enough to matter. Subsequent events proved that monetary policy really was potent. Possibly a little monetary restriction was insufficient but major restriction can seriously affect real economic activity.

THE 1980s

In the early 1980s the monetary brakes were applied very hard and they worked. Other commentators will be able to assess motivation and objectives. For example, it appears that the Bank of Canada succumbed once again to its old error of worrying more about the exchange rate than about its own domestic objectives. Many European governments allowed their currencies to depreciate against the United States dollar and this allowed their interest rates to fall below those of the United States. (The expected subsequent appreciation then compensated for the lower interest yield.) As a result, the monetary crunch was not so severe in these countries as it was in the United States. The Bank of Canada, however, supported the Canadian dollar and thus had to accept United States interest rates (plus an extra premium based on the difference between the United States and the Canadian inflation rates). Nonetheless, all countries' economies were hit by the severely restrictive monetary policy, give or take a bit, depending on how they rolled with the situation. As a result, the world fell into a really serious recession in 1981–2.

Was this process foreseen? Monetarists are a little hard to pin down on what they expected to be the costs of reducing inflation. It is clear to me, however, that the recession was longer and deeper and more generally upsetting to the economy than many monetarists thought it would be. Neo-Keynesians have been more open in documenting their views so there is no doubt that the inflation rate has come down somewhat faster than Nobel Laureate James Tobin (1980) or Data Resources President, Otto Eckstein (1981) predicted. In short, the actual costs of reducing inflation have come out somewhere between the predictions of the most pessimistic neo–Keynesians and of the most optimistic monetarists. It is clear that the inflation rate has fallen drastically in the United States and it seems to be falling also in Canada, although with quite a long lag.

Some of the costs were not expected at all, however, and these may turn out to be some of the most serious ones. The carefully built-up fabric of treaty-based rules and regulations designed to promote world trade has been put under heavy strain. For trading countries such as Canada, resurgence of beggar-my-neighbour trade policies can only be seen as a very serious development. Governments know that a round of trade restrictions is counter productive because every bit of gain to a protected import-competing industry is matched by a loss to an export industry. But pressures to preserve specific jobs by trade restrictions grows as a recession gets deeper and more prolonged. To resist this pressure is why nations tried to tie their own hands through such institutions as the GATT. The spectre of major trading countries such as Canada flirting with protectionist policies is testimony to the electoral pressures put on governments in times of severe recession.

What is the outlook for the near future? Will not enormous budget deficits ensure that inflation will break out again? I shall speak about the Canadian deficit which, although of unprecedented size, is nothing like as serious as it seems. First, much of it arises because of the inflation premium on interest rates. A 10 per cent inflation, for example, requires a 10 per cent payment from borrower to lender just to compensate for the erosion of capital due to inflation. If their real positions are not to be changed by the inflation, the borrower must pay, and the lender must 'save', the inflationary premium and add it to the nominal value of his capital. Furthermore, the borrower must borrow the inflation premium if he is to have his real position unaffected by the inflation. This is what evidence shows firms and households did in most countries during the 1970s and early 1980s. Firms borrowed to pay the inflation premium, thus holding their real indebtedness constant (measured in purchasing power terms) while households saved the inflation premium in order to maintain the real value of their stock of wealth. This is sound practice for firms and households and it is sound practice for governments. Indeed the howl of protest when the government followed the sensible policy of doing its accounting on a real, rather than a nominal, basis was quite amazing. Also, of course we must expect deficits in slumps and surpluses in booms, if the budget is to be balanced over the minimum sensible period, which is one business cycle.

There is some possibility that there is a structural problem in that the full employment balance may be unsatisfactory. (The uncertainty lies in estimating what the 'natural rate' of unemployment will turn out to be in the next recovery.) But, nevertheless, the bulk of the current deficit is a mixture of an inflationary and a recessionary problem, neither of which suggests that the resulting deficit will be a cause of further inflation.

WHAT HAVE WE LEARNED?

This has been a decade full of frustration. What if anything have we learned from it?

First, the view that monetary policy is an ineffective means of controlling demand is utterly discredited. Canadian gradualism failed in the 1970s for two main reasons.

1. Because it was an attempt to win the battle without taking casualties. Monetary restraint was applied so gently that there was plenty of time for other monetary instruments to take over from M1. Indeed the gradual decline in the rate of M1 growth was matched by a gradual increase in the rate of growth of M2.
2. The Bank of Canada failed to adjust its targets downwards when there was a major downward shift in the demand for M1 in the late 1970s. As a result money was not nearly so scarce *relative to the demand for it* (and, thus interest rates were not nearly so high) as one would have expected merely by looking at the data for the decelerating rate of M1 growth.

Monetary restraint 'failed' because monetary restraint was not really applied. When the world's economies were finally hit with some really severe monetary restraints in the early 1980s they responded appropriately by spiralling into a major recession. So we have learned that a sufficiently severe monetary restraint, with sufficiently high interest rates, can depress total demand by more or less any desired amount.

Secondly, those who argued that inflation was so stubborn that it would not respond significantly to demand restraint within a politically acceptable time horizon have also been shown to be wrong. From their point of view the actual behaviour of the American inflation rate can only be described as surprising — to say the very least.

Thirdly, the view that restrictive policy would act straight onto the inflation rate, leaving output and employment more or less unaffected, has been proven wrong. The economic wreckage of the last couple of years supports those who argued that the first effects of any anti-inflationary policy will be a decline in output and employment, and only after a long lag will the effects feed into a decline in the inflation rate.

There will be substantial argument about why the inflation

rate did not respond more quickly to restrictive monetary policy. Why did anti-inflationary policy begin by precipitating a really serious recession? Keynesians predicted this result on the basis of their theory of downward inertia in wage bargaining. Overlapping contracts plus concern over relative wages make workers very reluctant to respond to current market conditions when wages already in place cannot be changed. Rational-expectations theorists saw labour as being confused by what they read about the money supply in the financial press. As a result, they got their predictions of the inflation rate wrong and held their labour off the market in the mistaken belief that the real wage would turn out to be lower than in the event it actually was. These 'rational-expectations' explanations will not convince those who reject the new-Classical model. The explanations will, however, serve to keep alive the controversy about why the great recession was necessary before inflation began to moderate.

Fourthly, rigid control of a particular monetary aggregate along the lines urged by Friedman and his followers seems to me to have been discredited, although no doubt debate will continue interminably on this point. Shifts in the demands for monetary assets occur frequently. They take the form of substitution away from any monetary aggregate that is forced into short supply by the monetary authorities. Thus, we can expect as a matter of theory and experience that the velocity of circulation of any monetary aggregate that is controlled by the authorities will creep upwards. If the central bank is not allowed the discretion to adjust its monetary target downwards, an inflationary bias will be imparted into the system of monetary control. Econometric models are still a very imperfect tool and, as a result, the Bank of Canada will never be sure if it is faced with a permanent shift in the demand for money or a temporary aberration. If it is a permanent shift, time must pass before the new demand function can be estimated. As a result, effective monetary control is, and will always remain, an art rather than the simple, mindless policy that Friedman hoped to make it.

The above remarks apply to the Bank of Canada's type of policy where the interest rate is set so as to achieve the target money supply. Base control suffers from the same problems. The main transmission mechanism for monetary policy is through the excess demand functions for monetary assets onto interest rates and thence to spending. If demand functions for monetary assets that are subject to base-money reserve requirements should change, then there will be shifts in excess monetary demands and in interest rates and in spending without there being any change in the Bank's policy with respect to the monetary base.

Fifthly, the separation of the Bank of Canada from direct government control is on balance an advantage because it prevents a weak and irresolute government from reversing its course as soon as a restrictive monetary policy begins to hurt — as it must do if it is to be successful. On the other hand, the separation of control is a disadvantage because it results in confused signals. The Government of Canada repeatedly denied responsibility for the recession and expressed the belief that recovery was just around the corner. But if this were so, why should a union settle for a recession-induced, low-wage increase if good times are about to recur? The honest approach would have been to state that the tough times were induced by government policy and that they are going to continue until inflation was reduced. This, as well as being honest, gives a clear set of signals to labour and management who are trying to form expectations on which to base their wage-bargaining behaviour. As it was, the Canadian government must bear part of the blame for the strong wage inertia during 1981 and most of 1982. Wage settlements continued at very high rates in spite of high and rising unemployment while employers settled for high-wage contracts hoping that good times were just around the corner.

Sixthly, another reason for wage inertia that turned the anti-inflation crunch into a stagflation was a quite unexpected consequence of the very high interest rates that accompanied the tight monetary policy. High interest rates induced the recession as planned, but they also put firms into an extremely serious cash-flow position. As a result, when firms went to the bargaining table in 1981 and 1982 many of them found that a strike was a quick route to almost certain bankruptcy. Their cash-flow position would just not stand the loss of revenue tht accompanies a strike. To grant 'excessive' increases in wages was also a serious matter, but it did not betoken instant death. Firms could cut down on their employment (thus adding even more to unemployment), they could borrow more and they could hope that things would get better before the slow death caused by their excessive wage increases caught up with them. *Faced with a choice between instant death caused by a strike and slow strangulation caused by too-high wage increases, many firms chose the latter.*

Finally, a lesson I have learned but which is not widely disseminated is that the monetarist prescription for ending an inflation, reduce the rate of monetary expansion to what is consistent with the target inflation rate, is misguided in that it imposes an unnecessarily severe recession on the economy. Indeed, holding the rate of monetary expansion below the rate of inflation would, if the transition mechanism worked according to monetarist theory, guarantee a too-severe recession. Continually reducing the real money supply means continually lowering output and raising unemployment. Thus, to keep the rate of monetary expansion below the rate of price inflation until the inflation target is reached is to ensure (if the relationships hold up) that the recession will continue to get worse until the inflation target is met. Since it is now generally agreed that once an acceptably low rate of inflation has been achieved, there must be a once-and-for-all expansion in the real money supply the issue arises: why go through such a perverse path? The path suggested by standard macro theory is a once-for-all decrease in the real money supply to get a sufficient recession to induce the desired pressure on wage and price inflation – but no more. Ten per cent unemployment would probably have done the job in Canada making the additional unemployment a sheer waste.

WHAT WOULD WE LIKE TO KNOW MORE ABOUT?

Some parts of our recent performance still remain subject to real uncertainty. Here are two examples.

First, why did wage settlements moderate much faster in the United States than in Canada in the face of similar recessions? My own guess is that it is partly explained by different experiences in the 1970s. The United States economy was put through a major recession in 1974/75 that taught labour and management something about the trade-off between wages and jobs. Canadians, however, were shielded from this experience because wage–price controls, rather than market forces, were used to reduce wage inflation.

Secondly, what part did the Canadian government's 6–5 programme have in moderating inflation? This programme limited federal public sector wage increases to 6 per cent in 1983 and 5 per cent in 1984 and most provinces followed suit with similar, although not identical plans. My own guess is that it played a key part. Mrs Thatcher learned in 1979 that all the restraint in the world on the private sector may not stop an inflation if the public sector, unconstrained by any bottom-line considerations, goes off on a spree of acclerating wage settlements. There is no evidence that the Canadian public sector was leading private-sector wage inflation in 1980–2, but, having disciplined the private sector with demand restraint in 1982, it was necessary to get public-sector wages also under control to prevent them from becoming the leaders in further two-digit wage inflation.

THE RECOVERY

Natural market forces will sooner or later induce some recovery, but its timing and strength will be influenced by government policies. Monetary policy will affect the interest rate and the exchange rate. (A moderate depreciation of the Canadian dollar might, for example, could set off some export-led recovery.) Fiscal policy here, and in the United States, will be an important determinant of total demand.

The forthcoming recovery is going to provide one of the most critical tests to occur in economic theory in half a century. The theory to be tested is the theory that inflation is structurally built into the behaviour of our economy. If this theory is correct, inflation will break out once the recovery gets under way. Long before we get back to full employment two-digit inflation will recur and the whole costly anti-inflation experiment of the early 1980s will have been utterly in vain.

What are the reasons that lie behind this mind boggling possibility?

The first concerns the behaviour of imperfect product and factor markets. Once we return to full employment, so goes the theory, strong labour unions will push for increases in wages that will get them ahead of everyone else. Firms with market power will grant these wage increases in order to avoid work stoppages at times when demand and profits are high and will then pass these increases on in terms of higher prices. Other wage and price setters will then be dragged along more or less unwillingly in order to maintain some reasonable relation to the wage and price leaders. Once the others have adjusted, the leaders will try once again to push ahead, and another round in the wage-price spiral will be set in motion.

A second reason concerns the commitment of the government to full employment. Early Keynesians worried that the ability and willingness of governments to maintain full employment by demand management might remove the restraint on wage bargaining. If all governments are committed to create the demand needed to buy full employment output at any price level, what is to stop labour asking for too much, and firms granting it and then passing it on in higher prices? The only thing that wage and price setters need to worry about is not getting too far out of line with competitors. But imperfection of the links among markets in an oligopolistic (product and labour differentiated) world allows for lots of slack. When everyone is tending to err on the high side of the limits set by the need to remain competitive with each other, an inflationary bias can emerge from rounds of wage and price setting in spite of the constraints set by the need to worry about relative wages and prices.

The bout of really heavy unemployment in the 1980s was the first time since the 1930s that labour and management were presented with the consequences of a really serious recession. Possibly the government will have to allow such a recession to recur every now and then just to persuade labour and management that it is *not* prepared to underwrite any privately negotiated increases, no matter how inflationary they are. In this view, oligopolistic behaviour plus a government's commitment to full employment makes inflation inevitable.

The third alleged reason imparting a possible inflationary bias stems from the asymmetrical behaviour of wage costs and hence of prices. According to this theory, wages rise quickly in the face of excess demand and only fall slowly in the face of excess supply. This is the theory that lies behind the basic Keynesian assymetry where excess demand raises prices but excess supply lowers output. If so, an economy whose aggregate demand is fluctuating on either side of full employment will find prices rising in booms and output holding fairly steady, while output falls in slumps with prices holding fairly steady. This effect analysed by Gray and Lipsey (1974) imparts an inflationary bias to an economy whose fluctuations are centred on potential national income.

Another possible reason concerns people's loss of confidence in a stable price level. We do not know the effects of the end of the belief that to-day a buck is a buck and will remain a buck tomorrow. Now that people expect inflation, and now that institutions are adapted to inflationary expectations, the system's behaviour may be altered. We do not know in what ways it will be altered, but plausible sounding arguments are easy to develop suggesting that the alterations make the system more inflation prone.

Finally, there is a distinct possibility that the NAIRU (non-accelerating inflationary rate of unemployment) may have moved upwards as a result of the last recession. Although not a reason for permanent inflation, it may be a reason why the next recovery will generate an accelerating inflation. Business investment has been very low through the whole current slump period. Capital capacity may not then prove sufficient to employ 93 or 94 per cent of work force. There is a danger, therefore, that capital limitations will be encountered when there is still 8 or 9 per cent unemployment. If expansionary policies are applied in an effort to get unemployment down to 6 or 7 per cent, this will generate a demand inflation which could easily accelerate the inflation rate back to the two-digit range.

THE FORTHCOMING TEST

Of course economic theories do not get tested in any final sense. There is always room for doubt and multiple interpretations after any economic event. But the theory of secular inflation is very widely believed outside of the economics profession, and it has many adherents within the profession. Should the inflation rate bounce right back to two figures on the next recovery, this theory is going to be given a great boost.

It is important, therefore, that governments do not mismanage the forthcoming test. The theory that low inflation rates and something close to full employment *are* compatible should be given as good a run for its money as is possible.

Serious and hard thinking should be going on within governments on how this can be done. I do not have answers, but I do have an agenda of some of the topics that need thinking about and that need it urgently, *now*.

First, the recovery should be managed slowly rather than rapidly. A rapid reflation of the economy would risk the danger of seriously overshooting into the demand-inflation range, either because of lags or because the NAIRU turns out to be higher than policy-makers thought it was.

Secondly, there are no doubt many reforms that could be made on the wages front. Methods of controlling public sector wages need to be developed. Possibly some kind of comparability formulae (taking into account the many non-wage advantages that public-sector employees enjoy over those in the private sector) might allay fears that the public sector sometimes leads rather than follows private-sector wages. Compulsory arbitration might be abandoned, or at least changed so that the arbitrator must choose between the union's or the employer's last offer and cannot produce his own compromise. This system encourages both sides to make reasonable proposals and may reduce the number of disputes getting to the arbitration stage. Legislation might force annual bargaining by outlawing multi-year wage contracts. By making average wages more sensitive to current demand conditions, this system should reduce inertia when inflation is being decelerated and provide a quick warning of the development of excess demand pressures in the labour market when the economy is being expanded. This would not be an unmixed blessing and, as with all the other items on my list, this is only a suggestion for further thought and research.

Thirdly, the market rigidities that are introduced by such pro-monopoly bodies as agricultural marketing boards might be eliminated. I am afraid that this is nothing other than a pious hope. But it may be worth pointing out that, contrary to much of the rhetoric on the subject, the experience of other countries shows that such boards are not necessary to the survival of the agricultural sector. What they are probably necessary for is the survival of small-scale, inefficient agricultural units on the European pattern rather than large-scale, efficient units on the American pattern.

Fourthly, some hard thinking is needed to design better price indexes that properly state the real income loss from a rising price level. Base weighted indexes, such as the CPI, inevitably overstate the income compensation needed to restore real incomes after a general rise in prices in which the structure of relative prices also alters. Base weighted indexes assume that people blindly go on buying the same bundle of goods, whereas we know they substitute goods whose prices rise least for goods whose prices rise most, thus partially compensating for the real-income loss they would suffer if they left their consumption patterns unaltered.

Also, indexes need to be designed that do not include the effects of such 'real' shocks as changes in the terms of trade. A purely monetary shock requires that all prices and wages rise in the same proportion. Indexing can facilitate such adjustments. An adverse real shock, such as a rise in import prices relative to export prices, requires a fall in living standards which in turn requires that wages, salaries and other incomes rise less than prices. In these circumstances indexing can destabilize the system by setting up an unstable wage—price spiral. This was the British experience in the mid 1970s. Since some kinds of indexing are clearly here to stay, indices need to be devised that reduce the chances of setting up futile inflations in the face of shocks that cannot be indexed against because they lower average real living standards.

Finally, a series of deflationary supply-side shocks might be kept in reserve for use if the CPI were hit by some unexpected inflationary shocks during the upswing. Cutting of indirect taxes that feed directly into prices is an example. Doing this cannot stop inflation in the long run, but it can be used as a once-and-for-all measure to counter any upward shocks that hit the price level and might otherwise set off a wage—price spiral at or near full employment.

The next expansion of the world's economies will be the most important recovery since the one that ended the Great Depression. The earlier recovery tested and rejected the theory of *secular stagnation*: the theory that modern market economies had endemic depressionary tendencies. The forthcoming recovery will test the theory of *secular inflation*: the theory that market economies have endemic tendencies for inflation to accelerate at, or near, full employment.

What if the rate of inflation does accelerate back to the two-digit range as the world's economies recover? This outcome would be a very serious matter. Indeed, I doubt that our present free-market and collective-bargaining institutions would survive the conclusion that an inevitable concomitant of anything close to steady full employment was an *accelerating* rate of inflation.

Governments would then be faced with an unpalatable choice: accept an accelerating inflation rate or induce through tight monetary policy another recession, such as the one we have just witnessed, in order to break the inflation once again. This conclusion would be followed by an irresistible clamour for permanent intervention into wage—price setting. What would come out of such experiments we cannot predict now. Possibly something closer to a command economy with all of its well-known ridigities, inefficiencies and losses of personal freedom. Possibly some viable and not too restricting new institutions. Whatever the outcome, a serious experiment with permanent government intervention into wage and price setting is not something to be welcomed by those who believe that, relative to command economies, free markets are fairly efficient in allocating resources and decentralizing economic power.

Supporters of the free market must hope that the forthcoming test of the theory of secular inflation will have the same result as the earlier test of the theory of secular stagnation: theory tested and rejected. If instead the theory appears to pass the test, then we are all in for some very deep soul searching and hard work. The demand for permanent, anti-inflationary, government intervention will be hard to resist. We economists will then have to try to invent measures that will do the job with the minimum of destruction of market institutions for wage and price setting. It will not be easy and the results may be far from satisfactory. But if that is the way the world works, then we must somehow learn to live with it.

A far more unfortunate result would be if we *erroneously* accepted the theory of secular inflation. This is why it is so important that the next recovery be well managed. It is critical to give every chance for the economy to reach and stay at full employment without accelerating inflation. If the inflation rate is to accelerate, we want it to happen because the structural inflationary forces really are there, not because of avoidable policy errors.

On the verge of so important an economic experiment, we can only hope that macro policy makers realize the momentous times in which they are living and that they will prepare themselves by advanced planning and research to handle the upcoming crucial experiment as best they can.

BEYOND MONETARISM

Since picking the title for my paper, indeed since giving it, both the Federal Reserve and the Bank of Canada have abandoned monetary targeting, therefore, taking us into the post-monetarist stage rather more quickly than I had anticipated. (The collapse of conventional Canadian monetarism is brilliantly expounded by Courchéne (1983).)

Clearly, money things matter and clearly central banks must monitor monetary magnitudes. But rigid targets are, I feel, correctly discredited. Demand and supply functions shift as new innovations change the availability and attractiveness of various monetary assets. This is happening continuously and we must expect the electronics revolution to accelerate the pace of change. What after all is monetarism? Some see it as some mystical relation between the quantity of money and money national income. My reading of theory, and evidence, and my insistence on real behavioural relations, tells me that the main transmission mechanism is from interest rates to aggregate demand. Monetary policy works because it affects interest rates. But how does M1 and M2 targeting do this? It has to be that there is a stable demand function (and a whole set of other functions) such that the chosen magnitude, call it Mx, happens to track the inflation rate and varying Mx alters a real variable that actually affects the rate of interest. The actual causal nexus is from the rate of interest to the real economy, but Mx just happens to be a good indicator such that keeping Mx on track alters the rate of interest which alters aggregate demand so as to keep the inflation rate on track.

But there are countless behavioural relations in the link between Mx and the inflation rate. They can and do change. So rigid targeting is, and has been revealed to be, a poor policy. It may be better than even poorer, fine-tuning policies followed in earlier times, but that does not make it the best policy.

As Courchéne (1983) puts it:

Indeed, in a nutshell, the reason that the Bank abandoned the target range was precisely because it no longer felt that the demand for money was sufficiently stable to be a useful guide for changing monetary policy. The Bank recognized this as a possibility at the inception of monetary targeting: 'It should be borne in mind that M1 will provide useful information for policy purposes only so long as the public's behaviour with respect to its holdings of transactions balances per dollar of income continues to follow a reasonably predictable pattern. It is possible that the public's habits in this regard will change over time, perhaps in response to innovations in payments technology and in the characteristics of the various kinds of financial instruments offered by deposit-taking institutions and their close competitors.' In a word, this possibly became a reality. To see why this turned out to be the case is the purpose of the next section.

So Mx (in Canada's case M1) is targeted on because it provides information. But what really does the work is the interest rate. But, if M1 demand proves unstable enough so that it lacks sufficient informational content to provide a reasonable target, what can the Bank do? There is no point pretending that monetary policy is not an art; it is. So it seems to me that banks should look ultimately at the inflation rate. That is, after all, their monetary responsibility. Next they should worry about the GNP gap and unemployment. Monetarist and Keynesian inflation models agree that the GNP gap is the key variable influencing the sign of the change in the underlying inflation rate. (The rate may be strongly influenced by supply shocks and inertias but existing theories agree that the difference between actual and potential GNP is what is correlated with changes in the underlying inflation rate — in monetarist and new Keynesian theory it is the consequence of accelerating or decelerating inflation, in Keynesian theory it is the cause.) Then real interest rates should be studied as the influence on aggregate demand and hence the GNP gap. Then monetary aggregates should be looked at as an indication of what should be done to change interest rates so as to change demand so as to change the GNP gap, so as to change the inflation rate.

There is so much slippage in all of these relations that mechanical targeting makes little sense. Once fine tuning is abandoned, and the destabilizing effects of lags are fully understood in principle, then the best thing to do is to operate as an art. Worry about all variables. In 1972/73 the Bank of Canada was misled by the behaviour of unemployment, in 1979 it was misled by the behaviour of M1 demand. *Every informational variable is capable of deceiving.* The real underlying behavioural link, however, does not change, it is provided by the real interest rate.

So a central bank should watch all economic variables. In the end, it is the inflation rate that is its responsibility. Its main influence operates through interest rates on aggregate demand. That is the transmission mechanism it should keep firmly in view. But to control that, it must not get mesmerized by particular variables. It must form a balanced and hedged view based on every key variable available and the best theoretical and empirical evidence on how these are linked to the inflation rate.

But, if targeting on Mx is abandoned, will people not come to expect inflation? It is hoped that the risk of creating strong inflationary expectations can be minimized by a publically stated anti-inflationary policy on the part of the Bank: 'if the inflation rate accelerates, the monetary screws will be put on harder and harder until inflation comes down'. No commitment to an M1 target is needed. Just a commitment if the inflation rises, to put the screws on in terms of driving interest rates up and aggregate demand down using whatever quantitative restraints are needed on various monetary aggregates. All of this of course assumes that the theory of secular inflation does not pass the test. If it does, the main burden of anti-inflationary policy will have to pass out of the hands of the monetary authorities.

Central banking is an art. Let's admit it and practice it as such.

WAS IT WORTH IT?

Some say the great anti-inflationary war was too costly: I am not sure. I think it was somewhat more costly than it needed to have been — as are most wars. There certainly was a strong case for the imposition of wage—price controls in early 1981 to force the rate of wage and price inflation down to a level consistent with a drastically reduced rate of monetary expansion. If this had succeeded, much of the enormous human and material cost of the Great Recession would have been avoided. But if we learn to avoid the conditions that lead to future inflations because we now understand the high cost of eradicating them, the effort may have been worthwhile. Also, I do not know if the secular inflation theory is true or not. My neo-Classical colleagues know that it *is not* true. But my post—Keynesian colleagues know that it *is* true. Both groups seem to me to contain some pretty intelligent people. I do not know which group is right, but I shall look with great interest to see what we can learn from the next recovery. If I had to bet, it would be that the theory of secular inflation will be rejected as a dominating force, but that there will be a tendency for the inflation rate to drift upwards slowly due to the fundamental Keynesian asymmetry (prices rise faster in the face of excess demand than they fall in the face of excess supply). This tendency may have to be checked by occasional bouts of severe recession or, let us hope, some less-costly policy that is still but a gleam in the mind of some really creative economist. But only time will tell. In the meantime we must hope that recovery will come soon, so that no further large costs will be paid and that the inflation rate will stay down during the recovery so that it will not have been all in vain.

POSTSCRIPT

It is now 13 months since I gave my Killam Lecture and 9 months since I completed the final revisions for the version published above. Have we learned anything since then?

It seems to me that the most important event, because it was the most surprising to people who share the view of all the authors in this volume, was the speed with which the United States' inflation rate, followed by the Canadian rate, fell. One obvious explanation is that two of the industries that are key to wage inertia – cars and steel – had serious troubles that were secular rather than cyclical.

This suggests a really interesting conjecture. It is not unknown in intellectual history that an idea that has had to fight for recognition against all the forces of prejudice and intellectual conservatism has finally achieved recognition just when changed circumstances make it no longer relevant. Could this be the case with the neo- and post-Keynesian view of inflation?

The two pillars of the Keynesian theory of structural inflation are, first, firm and union power and, second, a policy commitment to full employment. Consider these in turn.

The industries that are looked to in the Keynesian view of wage and price setting are the traditional, smoke-stack industries of which autos and steel are typical. But these industries are in decline in all OECD countries. One of the statistics that always seems to me to encapsule this change is that in the United States the *increment* of employment in the fast food industry in the decade of the 1970s exceeded the total employment in the auto and steel industries! Employment is growing in services, in new, small-firm dominated manufacturing industries, in non-unionized sectors and in expanding areas such as the United States' sun belt and the Canadian West, where rigid wage and price setting practices are not heavily entrenched in long-established institutions. These industries may not impart the inflationary bias to wage and price setting that could have come from the established industries of the last three decades.

Then, we come to a major policy shift in the 1980s. The great recession of the early part of this decade may be seen as a very strong statement by governments that they no longer felt an absolute commitment to a policy of full employment. If governments make it clear that, for better or for worse, they are willing to tolerate major bouts of unemployment as a necessary cost of restraining inflation, the discipline that excessive wage demands may lead to loss of jobs is restored to labour markets.

There still remains the worry that micro-wage bargaining may create a wage—price leap-frogging spiral by the very dynamics of the micro-bargaining process, but this worry is much weakened by the two changes referred to above. Of course the only test of conflicting theories lies in actual experience. So we shall still wait with great interest to see the behaviour of wage setting as the current recovery proceeds.

A significant development seems to me to be the provision of further evidence on the shortcomings of strict monetarist rules. When interest rates tumbled from the 20—30 per cent range to single digit levels, there was a large, fully predictable increase in the demand for M1. This was re-enforced by a rise in transactions needs for money as the recovery proceeded. The Federal Reserve and the Bank of Canada accommodated these needs with rapid, temporary increases in the money supply. Milton Friedman, in a series of newspaper articles, has predicted a major outbreak of inflation and has pleaded for a return to a tight monetary policy. Had Friedman's advice been taken, the resulting money shortage would have sent interest rates soaring and probably nipped off the recovery. Friedman's advice shows up the weakness in the simple monetarist's position: they do not have an explicit theory of how the effects of changes in M are divided between changes in real income Y, and in the price level P when the initial position is not the economy's long-run equilibrium position. Friedman's policy arguments have assumed that all changes in M must show up in changes in P. This makes sense if we start from an equilibrium position where Y is at its potential level and the market rate of interest is at its long-term equilibrium level. But if we start, as we did in 1982 from a position where the rate of interest is extremely high and national income is well below potential, to insist on a long-term rule over the subsequent period of disequilibrium adjustment is to seriously inhibit the adjustment back to lower interest rates and higher income.

Of course central banks may mismanage the recovery in the future, but at the end of 1983 there was nothing to suggest that they were doing so currently.

REFERENCES

Barber, C. and McCallum, J. (1980) *Unemployment and Inflation: The Canadian Experience*. Toronto: The Canadian Institute for Public Policy.
Blinder, A. (1979) *Economic Policy and the Great Stagflation*. New York: Academic Press.

Canadian Public Policy, Supplement VII, April 1981.
Courchene, T. (1983) *The End of Monetarism*. Toronto: Howe Institute.
Eckstein, Otto (1981) *Core Inflation*. New Jersey: Prentice Hall.
Government of Canada (1975) *Attack on Inflation: A program of national action*. Ottawa.
Gray, M. and Lipsey, R. G. (1974) Is the natural rate of unemployment compatible with a steady rate of inflation? *Queen's University, Institute for Economic Research*, Discussion paper no.147.
Parkin, M. (1982) *Modern Macroeconomics*. New Jersey: Prentice Hall.
Tobin, J. (1980) Stabilization policy ten years after, *Brookings Papers on Economic Activity*, 1, 19–90.

4

Confusion in Economic Theory and Policy – Is There a Way Out?

WYNNE GODLEY*

THE POST-WAR KEYNESIAN CONSENSUS

It is a matter of record, not opinion, that the first 25 years after the Second World War was a period of unprecedented and almost unqualified success, at least for the developed countries, with respect to all the matters of major concern in the conduct of macroeconomic policy. There was nearly continuous expansion of real income and output, and even those countries which grew relatively slowly still grew fast enough to more than double their standard of living in the quarter century. Poverty, which had afflicted whole classes and regions before the war, was substantially eliminated. Unemployment only existed for short periods except in a few unfortunate regions within countries. Inflation was generally below 5 per cent per annum except during quite short and unusual episodes such as the Korean war.

The policy makers of that era and those who advised them particularly in Britain and the United States came, generally speaking, to share a view, the authorship of which was correctly attributed to Keynes, that governments could, and therefore should, accept responsibility for ensuring real growth and full employment. And those same people also believed that the success, at that time, of the industrialized economies was the consequence of the implementation of Keynesian policies.

While the idea that governments can and should accept responsibility for maintaining full employment can be attributed to Keynes, the theoretical basis of the explicit or implicit models

---

* I am grateful to Francis Cripps and Terry Ward for reading through my drafts and making many helpful suggestions.

used *in practice* to underpin Keynesian policy advice was pretty crude. The essential points were as follows.

1. To obtain real growth and full employment it was necessary and sufficient to expand aggregate demand for goods and services. Governments could achieve this by expanding their own expenditure on goods and services or releasing disposable income by cutting taxation.
2. There might be a temporary constraint on the growth of real output imposed by shortage of physical or human capital. A constraint might also be imposed if exports did not rise sufficiently to pay for imports.
3. Subject to these constraints, fiscal policy could safely adopt full employment as a target while disregarding any imbalance in the Budget — that is, any excess of public spending measured in nominal terms over revenue receipts.
4. Monetary policy under this system of ideas did not matter much, the quantity of money itself being a residual number thrown up by everything else that happened which could safely be ignored. It was even the case through much of the post-war period that statistics relating to what are now called 'monetary aggregates' (the stock of money and various other financial assets) were not regularly available, if at all.[1]

There was no *economic* theory of inflation in this scheme of things. Indeed inflation was generally thought to be a largely indeterminate process in which social and political factors played a large role and which could only be avoided by good luck or, conceivably, by skilful political intervention in the form of incomes policies and so on. This was the view taken by Keynes himself at least when, late in his life, he was considering the problems which would in practice arise in the attempt to maintain full employment after the war. Thus in 1944 he wrote: 'the task of keeping efficiency-wages reasonably stable (I am sure that they will creep up steadily in spite of our best efforts) is a political rather than an economic problem' and 'One is also, simply because one knows no solution, inclined to turn a blind eye to the wages problem in a full employment economy.'[2]

I had better come clean at this stage and admit that, as a civil servant employed full time during the 1950s and 1960s on macroeconomic analysis, it was my belief that the simple system of ideas outlined in the paragraphs above was nearly sufficient by way of economic theory for macroeconomic policy purposes.

It seemed to me then that while macroeconomic models and the execution of policies more or less based on them could be marginally improved, all the theoretical problems which had any serious bearing on practical matters had been substantially solved. Progress in economic management was to be made through the patient and systematic accumulation of information, which could then be used to improve the detailed execution of policy; it could be used, for instance, to improve the way in which public expenditure was planned so as to improve public services, to reduce regional inequalities, to increase industrial efficiency and so on. Any significant aberration from full employment, I believed, or even any actual or potential international imbalance of a commercial or financial kind could and would quite safely and quickly be patched up.

This brief characterization of the immediate post-war consensus and my own view about it would be incomplete without acknowledging that there was always an undercurrent of passionate dissent. This came from people who resented the Keynesian assumption that governments have an essential role to play in managing modern economies; to them the ideas that governments could borrow with impunity and that 'money did not matter' was intellectually and morally rebarbative. The same people held the view that rates of inflation which occurred at that time were unacceptably high. And it would be wrong to say or insinuate that 'monetarism' was just a politically motivated movement based on a particular set of value judgements. It contained, in particular, three lines of argument which came to be extremely influential in the subsequent academic debate. First, monetarism, unlike 'crude' Keynesian doctrine, claimed to give a comprehensive explanation of inflation as well as a cure for it. Secondly the monetarists had at the centre of their system of ideas a postulate about the *stock* of money and the *flow* of income. Thirdly they attached great importance to the long-run consequences of policy, objecting strongly to the attempts made by governments to 'fine tune' — that is to adopt stabilization policies with a very short time horizon.

Probably in the post-war period there was much more dissent from the Keynesian orthodoxy than appeared at the time. However, this dissent, whether coming from politicians, academics, businessmen or others, was neutralized for years simply because of the manifest and, as I have already said, almost unqualified success which Keynesian policies enjoyed.

DEPRESSION, INFLATION AND MACROCONFUSION IN THE 1970s AND 1980s

Since the early 1970s we have seen a chronic and, on the whole, deepening depression throughout the world accompanied by greatly accelerated inflation.

In Britain total real output rose only about 1 per cent per annum on average between 1973 and 1979, unemployment rose from 2½ per cent to 5½ per cent and prices rose on average by 15 per cent per annum. Between 1979 and 1983, notwithstanding rapidly rising production of oil, total output has *fallen* absolutely, unemployment has more than doubled again, reaching over 3 million in mid 1983, while the average rate of inflation has been 11 per cent per annum over the 4-year period taken as a whole though it has recently been falling.

It is extremely difficult to understand or even characterize the violent changes in opinion and in the policy stance of governments throughout the world that have occurred during this period. What I say now may look quite wrong in a few years time. I shall briefly discuss first some of the main features of the academic discussion; then speculate about the revolution in political opinion.

THE ACADEMIC DISCUSSION

Why was it that Keynesian economists were thrown so emphatically on the defensive from the early 1970s onwards?

I think there are two main reasons which have strong interrelationships between them.

The first can be stated very simply. As I have already pointed out, the Keynesian system of ideas did not contain a strong theory of inflation. This could pass while inflation was extremely low. But when it moved into double figures and threatened to accelerate further the view of inflation as a largely contingent process, often arising more or less by accident because of changes in the political temperature to be cured if at all by some kind of incomes policy, looked impoverished and impotent. The rapid acceleration of inflation was widely thought within as well as outside the profession to have disproved the Keynesian 'institutional' view of inflation.

The second reason for the poor showing of the Keynesians

was that what had become traditional macroeconomic theory was undergoing a very thorough process of reformulation from inside itself. The internal upheaval started in the mid 1960s, before the monetarist counterrevolution became really effective and stemmed from deep contradictions in the logic of the Keynesian system which could have been diagnosed at any time since the publication of the *General Theory*. I shall attempt, in the rest of this section, to characterize this upheaval.

The elementary Keynesian textbook exposition says that the national income flow (in 'equilibrium') is equal to non-income related expenditures (typically fixed investment and government spending) times a 'multiplier'. The size of the multiplier is determined by personal savings and taxation, which are 'leaks' out of the aggregate income flow. At the same time the stock of money must be willingly held — and this will only happen, given the aggregate income flow, at one rate of interest. Therefore, with fixed investment at least in part determined by the rate of interest, it becomes possible to infer an 'equilibrium' for the whole economic system conditional on the government's fiscal and monetary policy and the parameters of the investment, consumption and demand for money functions.

Such is the essential character of the IS—LM apparatus which has lain at the heart of Keynesian macroeconomic theory ever since the influential article which Hicks[3] published in 1937.

One contradiction within this system has been known for years. If fixed investment is positive (as it must be if it is to drive all or part of the system) then the stock of capital must be increasing. But then the solution of the IS—LM equations cannot be an equilibrium after all because with a constant income flow the stock of capital must be increasing indefinitely. The contradiction is actually quite clear for everyone to see in the *General Theory* itself, since this explicitly assumes the stock of capital to be given while making fixed investment, i.e. a *change* in the stock of capital, the driving force of the economy.[4]

Macroeconomic theorists managed for years to ignore this problem, sometimes by turning a blind eye and sometimes explicitly with the excuse that they were only describing 'short-term' equilibrium.

It is a bizarre fact about the history of Keynesian macroeconomics that the subject was thrown into prolonged convulsions by the 'discovery'[5] in the mid 1960s of nothing other than an accounting identity — the logical equivalence (in a closed economy) between the budget deficit and the private-sector financial surplus; this had the logical implication that a budget deficit generates a growing net stock of financial assets. In other words, it was suddenly discovered that the solution of the IS—LM system failed to qualify as a genuine equilibrium, not only because it allows the stock of fixed capital to rise indefinitely relative to income, but also because it allows the stock of government debt (and therefore the net stock of private financial wealth) to rise indefinitely as well.

When they realized the significance of the flow-of-funds identity, Keynesian theorists did not abandon the IS—LM apparatus. On the contrary, they retained the basic IS—LM system of equations but modified it by making the stock of private wealth an argument of the consumption function in addition to disposable income. They also were more ready, on a parallel argument, to make the stock of capital itself an argument of the investment function.

These modifications to the core equations of the Keynesian model do imply that, given the government's economic-policy decisions, if an economy moves eventually to equilibrium it will be a full equilibrium in which all stocks as well as all flows are determinate and constant. But while this may sound quite simple, the comparative static framework habitually used required a lot of complex and opaque mathematical paraphernalia to establish the precise nature of the stability conditions which would ensure that equilibrium was ever reached at all.

One of the most important contributions to this discussion was an article published in 1973 by Blinder and Solow[6] entitled 'Does fiscal policy matter'? The authors concluded that fiscal policy probably did influence the aggregate real-income flow but only as the outcome of a process too complex to have found its way even now into the mainstream textbooks and, in its substance, qualified by the probability that there would be 'crowding out' effects through negative feedbacks on private spending from the monetary system.

An article which is equally important in the history of this debate is that by Tobin and Buiter.[7] They reach substantially the same conclusion as Blinder and Solow but the old Keynesian self confidence is looking very sickly indeed. Tobin and Buiter describe their work as 'a theoretical exercise addressed to a rather esoteric and artificial question in the logic of aggregate demand.

Confusion in Economic Theory and Policy

Does expansionary fiscal policy raise aggregate demand permanently or at best only temporarily?'

What question, I must ask, could be less esoteric and artificial? After this introduction, coming from leading champions of the Keynesian tradition, the reader must feel entitled at least to call into question whether indeed fiscal policy can be effective other than temporarily.

At all events, one consequence of this debate has been to focus a great deal of discussion within the Keynesian tradition onto the following problem. Fiscal policy can only increase the aggregate income flow by raising the total stock of financial assets as the budget goes into deficit. Suppose now that the monetary authorities, instead of 'accommodating' the expansion, are determined to keep the stock of money (i.e. a subcategory of the total stock of financial assets) on a predetermined path irrespective of the fiscal policy, what then will be the outcome?

It is easy to show, once the problem is set up in these terms, that fiscal expansion may be partly or wholly ineffective in changing the aggregate income flow since public expenditure, in the long run, will at least to some extent 'crowd out' private expenditure.

But with this much conceded the academic discussion had pretty well slipped into a night in which all the cows were black. The Keynesians no longer had clear and effective arguments to withstand the monetarist counterrevolution. As I have already pointed out the monetarists claimed to have a comprehensive explanation of inflation; they had always attached great importance to stock flow norms as well as to the long-run implications of short-term policies.

Following the greatly accelerated inflation rates at the beginning of the 1970s there has been a revolution (and much confusion) in the way governments have conducted a policy which matches this ferment in the academic discussion.

Thus it came to be accepted by governments that the long-run effects of an expansionary fiscal policy on real output and unemployment were uncertain and probably perverse, while the effect of monetary policy on inflation would be rather certain and rapid. A new and crucial role was given to 'controlling the money supply' and fiscal policy was in theory subordinated to this objective. These principles have generally been sponsored by central banks and some of the main international organizations (e.g. the

IMF though not, to its credit, the OECD) because of the supposed connection between monetary expansion and subsequent inflation; and also because markets are supposed to have been 'taught' that rapid monetary expansion will lead to high interest rates which will block economic expansion.

THE PUBLIC DISCUSSION AND THE POLITICAL MOOD

My perspective on the political mood is strongly influenced by having worked as a *conjoncturiste* in the British Treasury throughout the Keynesian heyday, that is, from 1956 until 1970. I have it burnt into my mind that there was a political crisis in 1958 when unemployment rose to 2 per cent; that public opinion was outraged when unemployment reached 2½ per cent in 1962; that when unemployment reached 4 per cent in 1972 there was talk in high places of civil war; and that in each of these episodes the (Conservative) government of the time was forced to make a violent change in the direction of revising aggregate demand by fiscal and monetary expansion.

In 1983 we have, in Britain, unemployment in excess of 12 per cent (over 3 million) and rising. Yet public opinion has now accepted that this is not the result of government policy at all. In so far as any policy is to blame, it is (supposed to be) the policy of the previous period, which tried to reduce unemployment below some 'natural' rate; even maybe there is indeed no such thing as involuntary unemployment after all with the implication that the government could not do anything.

Why has this happened? I find it hard to believe that it has much to do with the thoughts and writings of academics.

Perhaps people were frightened by the unprecedentedly high rates of inflation which occurred in the early 1970s, bringing ruin to a few and uncertainty to everyone; perhaps they strongly resented the growing tendency of trade unions selfishly to exploit their monopoly power with much smug self importance. But this does not seem enough to explain the violent change of mood.

As to what has happened to the political mood rather than why, I think it is important to put things into a historical perspective.

Here I have recourse again to Keynes, not the theoretician, but the brilliantly rhetorical writer who could look at the real world with subtle intuition, flair and penetrating understanding. Consider the following passage from a radio talk in 1934, 'Poverty in plenty: Is the economic system self-adjusting'. Here he adopts a position far more radical than appears in the *General Theory*; it amounts to a root and branch rejection of economic theory. He said:

> On the one side are those who believe that the existing economic system is, in the long run, a self-adjusting system, though with creaks and groans and jerks, and interrupted by time lags, outside interference and mistakes ... on the other side of the gulf are those who reject the idea that the existing economic system is, in any significant sense, self-adjusting. ...
>
> The strength of the self-adjusting school depends on its having behind it almost the whole body of organised economic thinking and doctrine of the last hundred years. This is a formidable power. It is the product of acute minds and has persuaded and convinced the great majority of the intelligent and disinterested persons who have studied it. It has vast prestige and a more far-reaching influence than is obvious. For it lies behind the education and the habitual modes of thought, not only of economists, but of bankers and businessmen and civil servants and politicians of all parties. ...
>
> Thus, if the heretics on the other side of the gulf are to demolish the forces of nineteenth-century orthodoxy ... they must attack them in their citadel. No successful attack has yet been made. ...
>
> I range myself with the heretics.[8]

In other words, what is at issue is a conflict far wider and older than one between contemporary schools of economic theory today. It is between two whole approaches to political economy corresponding to casts of mind as mutually irreconcilable as metaphysics to empiricism or religion to humanism.

The division noted by Keynes between those who postulate a self-regulating economic system (which if allowed to operate without interference will produce optimum results), and those who see the evolution of the economic system as a highly contingent historical process (in which more or less anything can happen), where economic policy at a national and international level has an absolutely crucial role to play, is very old. It was bitterly manifest throughout nineteenth-century England. Many political economists who were personally good men sponsored what now seems obviously to be an incredibly inhumane system. There were children who never left their place of work. Cobbett[9] writing in 1826 said: 'Dogs and hogs and horses are treated with more civility [than the workers] and as to food and lodging how gladly would the workers change with them.' Disraeli writing in 1827 pilloried the attitude of the Political Economists to the Poor

Laws. He describes how the hero of one of his early novels, Popanilla, was accosted by a crippled beggar who had a wife and twelve small children. He was about to give him some money, 'but his companion repressed his unphilosophical facility. "By no means!" said his friend, who turning round to the beggar, advised him, in a mild voice, to *work*.' It was *laissez-faire* as a positive doctrine which sponsored the export of food from Ireland during the famine. It was *laissez-faire* which sponsored mass unemployment in the 1930s and which sponsors it again today.

It is thanks to a humanitarian movement based on the ideas of a few great eccentric thinkers such as Wilberforce and Keynes (in his capacity as political adviser and commentator) who, rejecting economic theory and looking at the real world, could see that certain features of it were intolerable, and simply had to be changed.

In some letters written by Keynes towards the end of his life he spoke of *laissez-faire* as though it was an illness. For instance, in 1944 he wrote to J. M. Fleming, 'I sometimes think that when a post mortem is carried out on you and James [Meade], all kinds of pockets of *laissez-faire* appendicitis will be found in unsuspected parts of the body.'

It is important not to be historically parochial about the controversies which have raged around economics and economic policies during the last 10 years.

> And what there is to conquer
> By strength and submission, has already been discovered
> One or twice, or several times, by men whom one cannot hope
> To emulate — but there is no competition —
> There is only the fight to recover what has been lost
> And found and lost again and again: and now under conditions
> That seem unpropitious.[10]

I can only end this section of my talk by making a straightforward *protest* against the view that in the 1980s real economic systems (conceived on a world, country or regional basis) are self adjusting; and living in a country where many industrial areas have been laid waste by prolonged and severe recession, and where as a consequence there are few workplaces left, that all unemployment is, in any useful sense, voluntary.

A PERSONAL EVALUATION

What to make of the predicament and the confusion which surrounds it?

Having protested against the prevailing morality I am prepared to assert that the macroeconomic theory on which policy was based in the successful post-war period was essentially correct after all.[11] Now, as then, a necessary condition for the expansion of real demand, output and employment is that fiscal policy should be expansionary, although the scale of the resulting demand expansion must be kept within the limits set by productive potential if inflationary pressure is to be mitigated. There is no intrinsic reason now, any more than in the 1950s and 1960s, why relatively full employment should be inconsistent with inflation on a scale which most people will find acceptable. Now, as before, the effect of fiscal policy on real demand, output and employment can be rapid and permanent while its effect on inflation is slow and uncertain.

I do not for a moment accept that the post-war Keynesian consensus has been in any way confuted by *events*. In Britain the first phase of the recession was generated by a loss of real income because of the rise in commodity prices (including oil) in 1973 and 1974, reinforced by the restrictive fiscal policies generally adopted by the Labour Government in 1975. The rise in prices during that period was not caused by monetary factors at all but by the rise in commodity prices (including oil) gravely compounded at least in Britain by a most unfortunate 'threshold' scheme which probably added 10 per cent per annum to the rate of wage inflation compared with what otherwise would have happened from 1975 onwards. Since 1979 the recession has been turned into a slump by another bout of fiscal and monetary disinflation which cut domestic demand and also, because the policy caused the real exchange rate to rise rapidly, cut foreign demand as well. Similar factors account readily for comparable developments elsewhere in the world.[12]

On the other hand recent events have, I think, gone strongly against the monetarist story at least as told a few years back. The fact that the monetarists won the argument in the 1970s does not mean they were right.

Whatever the rhetoric, events have not been at all in line with what our government expected. When they came to power in mid 1979 it was clear, right in line with the counsel of their monetarist advisers, that they expected the effect of their policies on prices to be rapid and permanent and the effect on unemployment to be small and temporary. Ever since November 1980 our Ministers have even been purporting to see signs of recovery. And in the spring of 1982, just before a significant reacceleration in the rate of unemployment, our Financial Secretary, Mr Leon Brittan, made the notorious and fatuous claim that, 'the signs of recovery are all about us and only the most blinkered pessimist can fail to see them'.

The fact that the British Government's predictions about the industrial depression have been so wrong while the reduction in inflation is clearly the consequence not of controlling the money supply 2 years previously (when it rose particularly fast) but of high unemployment and a high rate of exchange, should surely have led them to question the whole basis of what they are doing.

Neither in their words nor in their deeds is there yet any evidence that this is what they are doing.

THE FUTURE

Even if I am correct in supposing that the post-war Keynesian system of ideas was a basically correct foundation for economic policy this does not, unfortunately, mean there is a simple solution to the problem of world recession by simply reverting to old ways. Even if my views about the key role of fiscal policy were generally accepted and monetary targeting were abandoned, the world economic situation has now gone so badly wrong that it would be very difficult to put things right again. To achieve sustained growth would require that countries cooperate with one another in an altogether new way, coordinating their plans as they have never done before.

Consider what would happen if there was such a change of mood that all governments suddenly agreed that fiscal expansion across the world was after all a necessary condition for increasing the level of output and reducing unemployment.

Here are some of the problems.

First, since different countries are in different degrees of recession and also a very long way from full employment, they would have to converge towards full employment at different rates. A 'locomotive' process of expansion is theoretically feasible but what you have to imagine (in the analogy of my colleague Francis Cripps) is a train where the engine is travelling at a different speed from the carriages and indeed where all the carriages are moving at different rates from one another. This postulates a very high degree of underlying knowledge and a very high degree of cooperation.

An analogous problem arises because of very disparate performances in international trade between the various industrial countries.

Even without the world recession structural imbalances in international trade would in any case have been arising particularly in Britain and the United States but also in the EEC taken as a whole, because of the extremely rapid penetration of domestic markets mainly by Japan and certain other newly industrialized countries.

The scale of the potential imbalances has certainly been greatly aggravated by the erratic and often perverse movements of exchange rates. Thus the underlying (or 'high employment') current account deficits of Britain and the United States must now be much worse than they otherwise would have been because very high real interest rates (and in Britain North Sea oil combined with relatively severe recession) has caused exchange rates to rise to levels which can only be called absurd.

The conclusion must be that even if we could now coordinate fiscal policies to accommodate the fact that different countries are in different degrees of recession, I am quite sure that very large current-account imbalances would emerge. So we need not only to coordinate our fiscal policies, we also need to coordinate our trade policies and payments as well. Yet, under the present system of floating exchange rates, we have been deprived of the traditional means of making balance-of-payments adjustments. Paradoxically, by having floating exchange rates we have deprived ourselves of exchange rates as an instrument of economic policy.

In sum, I believe that there is no intrinsic reason why growth and full employment in the industrialized world should not be achieved by coordinated fiscal policies in combination with an appropriate configuration of exchange rates. The difficulties are first that action and cooperation along these lines are not at all what governments at present have on their agenda; second there does not at present exist a system of information and analysis which could form the basis for such a coordinated plan of action; third, even if exchange rates could be adjusted to satisfy the long-run conditions for equilibrium, the trade responses to currency adjustment are known to be very slow so there would be a long transitional period during which potential-deficit countries would have to suffer large increases in import prices (and therefore inflationary pressure) and cuts in real income.

I am, therefore, very doubtful if, even supposing that international cooperation was attempted, it could now really be successful without some form of international trade management. By trade management I do *not* mean protection in the sense ordinarily understood, i.e. a situation where individual countries unilaterally protect individual weak industries without international agreement and in a way unrelated to general macroeconomic management.

What I have in mind is that deficit countries adopt the kind of protection specifically catered for in the little read and, I believe, never used Article 12 of GATT which is specifically designed to make full employment possible in countries which would otherwise be subject to a general balance-of-payments constraint. The key point of such trade management would be, first, that it would be operated as a macroeconomic instrument, in harmony with fiscal policy, so as to ensure that the balance of payments would not be any more favourable than would otherwise be the case; in other words such protection would be used entirely to make possible higher domestic production — reducing the import propensity without reducing total imports themselves below what they otherwise would be. Under such conditions the rest of the world does not suffer (its exports being, by assumption, fully maintained) and the recovery of output can be much more rapid and less inflationary.

I think it worth quoting Keynes on this subject in the belief that his practical insights here as elsewhere were essentially sound. He wrote to J. M. Fleming

> I am not one of the 'most economists' [who believe] that... disequilibrium ought, so far as possible, to be corrected by movements in the rate of exchange rather than by controls over commodity trade.
>
> There is, first of all,... the simple-minded argument that, after all, restriction of imports does do the trick, whereas movements in the rate of exchange do not necessarily do so.
>
> ...
>
> There are two objections to movements in the rate of exchange,.... The first relates to the effect on the terms of trade.... in certain conditions of the

elasticities involved, a depreciation in the rate of exchange may actually worsen the balance of payments, and it is easy to imagine cases where, even if equilibrium is restored, it is at the cost of a serious and unnecessary reduction in the standard of life.

In the second place, in the modern world, where wages are closely linked with the cost of living, the efficacy of exchange depreciations may be very considerably reduced.

Apart, however, from these two arguments, the preference in favour of movements in the rate of exchange seems to me to be based on a vestigial belief in the way in which things would work under *laissez-faire*, ... [13]

What about inflation? I have no time to do more than record my disbelief that any sustained recovery to tolerably high levels of employment would cause accelerating inflation. That it necessarily does is *disproved* by the fact that we did have, in Britain, a period of 15 years (1950–65) when there was no unemployment (it averaged less than 2 per cent) with low and non-accelerating inflation and I see no reason, particularly if the expansion were handled with a high degree of political flair, why this should not happen again. Nothing has happened to my conviction that Keynes was right to diagnose inflation as an essentially political problem to be dealt with by political means. If there was a moderate increase in the rate of inflation (without it accelerating indefinitely) I would regard this as a small price to pay for full employment.

There is a danger that in the event of sustained expansion, inflation and financial instability will arise from a renewed energy shortage as well as from higher commodity prices in general. To some extent it is possible to mitigate these dangers by forward planning now. Thus energy conservation remains important even though we are experiencing a temporary glut. And I am still convinced that the creation of buffer stocks now could mitigate the inflationary effect of a rise in commodity prices should this threaten world recovery.

I therefore end on a note of optimism but one so heavily qualified that it can scarcely be heard. To use the last paragraph of the book[14] I have just written with Francis Cripps:

We believe that it is possible for the world to achieve, once again, sustained real growth with high employment. Inflation might then be more rapid although this is not inevitable. Yet we cannot hope even to see the beginnings of such a recovery until the peoples and governments of the world are convinced that the achievement is indeed within their power, and work together towards coordinated growth based on expansionary fiscal and trade policies that are mutually compatible.

TECHNICAL APPENDIX

I referred in my paper to contradictions at the heart of Keynesian theory. In this appendix I attempt to set out rigorously, if briefly, what these are and suggest a means by which they can be resolved.[15]

If only the Keynesian model had started off life with the national income flow identity properly embedded in a system of balance sheets recording stocks of assets and liabilities at the beginning and end of each accounting period! It is as though commercial accounting was limited to the use and compilation of appropriation accounts without there being balance sheets to check the accuracy of the flow transactions and tell firms where, at any point of time, they have got to.

If explicit consideration had been given by Keynes to stock variables as well as flow variables the primeval equation system at the heart of macroeconomics would surely have been different. I suggest it might, and certainly should, have been as follows.[16]

We start with the *General Theory* assumptions that the economy is closed and has no fiscal system and add the assumptions that there is a commercial banking system and that all money is credit money. The system of balance sheets recording the progress of such an economy would show the total stock of financial assets (credit money in the simplest case) always exactly equal to total financial liabilities (bank loans). It would also show a stock of tangible assets, part of which would be collateral for the loans.

Only now are we in a proper position to consider the usual starting point, the national income flow identity, because it should comprise compatible concepts such that flows have consistent counterparts in the balance sheets.

In view of the balance-sheet system the natural classification of expenditure flows is now not into consumption and investment but into loan-financed expenditure (a flow which in each period is equal to the change in bank loans recorded in balance sheets as accounting between the beginning and end of the period) and income-financed expenditure (the difference between this and income being equal to the change in the stock of financial assets).

With a coherent accounting system set up so as to make possible simultaneous consideration of stocks and flows, the income

Confusion in Economic Theory and Policy

expenditure multiplier equalizes, not savings and investment, but the creation of debt (which arises whenever there is loan-financed expenditure) with the demand for financial assets. Thus loan-financed expenditure is the driving force; the bank loans which are its counterpart create simultaneously an addition to the stock of financial assets (money in the simplest case) and an initial addition to the income flow of exactly equal size. Then the multiplier will ensure that aggregate income expands on whatever scale ensures that the stock of assets is willingly held. The creation of debt is exogenous but the stock of financial assets is endogenous in the sense that it can be represented as a function of current and lagged income.

The crucial point is this. We no longer need the rate of interest to bring the supply of credit into equality with the demand for assets since the aggregate income flow will do this at any rate of interest.

And changes in aggregate income will have been generated by the changing stock of debt, not via a monetarist black box, but through a good old Keynesian multiplier.

FISCAL POLICY IN A STOCK EQUILIBRIUM MODEL[17]

When this stock equilibrium model is extended to comprise fiscal policy, unlike the pure flow model above, its properties are radically changed. The enclosing of all flows within a consistent system of balance-sheet constraints leads naturally to the conclusion that fiscal policy, properly defined, uniquely determines the aggregate income flow, the effects of monetary policy necessarily being transitory.

I start, again, with the accountancy of stocks and flows when there is a fiscal system. The system of balance sheets must be expanded to include government debt along with the private debt among total liabilities, so that total financial assets held by the (non-bank) private sector will now be equal to the sum of public and private debt; this implies that total government debt must always be identically equal to total financial assets less total private debt. And the national income flow system must now comprise government expenditure and net government income defined consistently so that the difference between these two flows is always exactly equal to the change in government debt outstanding in any period considered.

In attempting to characterize verbally how such a system will function I shall for purely expositional reasons describe all processes in terms of adjustments to stationary equilibria. The analysis of all such processes can readily be adapted to represent continuous change by supposing that the economic system is always undergoing a series of overlapping adjustments caused by changes in the government's fiscal and monetary policy in successive periods. I do *not* believe that economic systems ever in reality achieve conditions of stationary equilibrium. Indeed my essential concern here is with the dynamics of an everlasting transition towards continuously changing, and therefore purely hypothetical, stationary equilibria.

How then is the aggregate income flow determined? My first contention is that the driving force, as in the simpler case where there was no fiscal system, is the creation of debt — the sum now of public and private debt. That is to say, private and public loan expenditure generate debts thereby simultaneously creating financial assets on an exactly equal scale. Then, whatever may be the rate of interest, the aggregate income flow ensures, via a Keynesian multiplier, that the private sector willingly holds these financial assets. The stock of assets is endogenous to the system determined (at any given rate of interest) as a function of current and lagged disposable income. So also is the stock of money, a sub-category of the total of financial assets, endogenously determined.

How is it that the income flow is uniquely determined by fiscal policy? The conditions for stationary equilibrium are set out in Fig. 4.1 (devised by K. Coutts).

The vertical scale above the point marked zero measures stocks of financial assets less private debt, which, as we have seen, is equal by definition to government debt. Below the zero point the vertical scale represents flows (per unit of time) of government expenditure (G) and taxes net of interest payments (T). At the point marked zero on the vertical scale the horizontal line measures the national income flow along the horizontal axis.

Government expenditure is treated as exogenous. Taxes are shown as an increasing function of income conditional on a family of progressive tax rates. The intersection between G and T shows the level of income at which the budget is balanced.

The curved diagonal line in the top right quadrant measures desired stocks of financial assets. These rise as total income rises

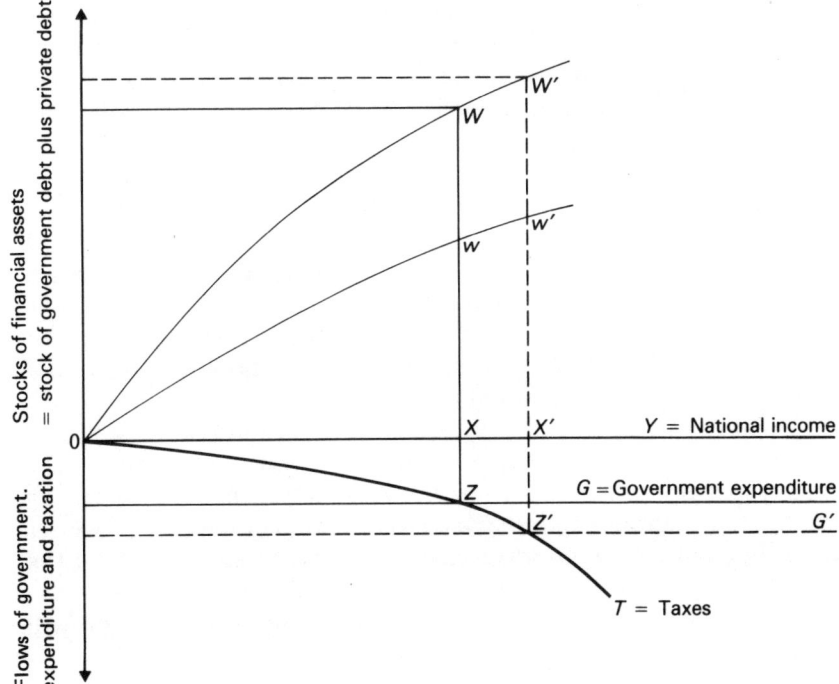

Figure 4.1 *Stationary equilibrium on alternative assumptions about fiscal policy and asset norms. (The curved lines, 0w, represent desired stocks of assets.)*

but at a decelerating rate since asset norms are assumed to exist relative to disposable income.

Consider first a point of full stationary equilibrium where the national income flow is given by the point of intersection X; here the budget is balanced ($G = T$) and therefore no change is occurring in government debt. This is also a point of asset equilibrium for the private sector indicated by the intersection W.

Now suppose that government expenditure rises from G to G'. The impact effect will be to increase stocks of government debt (because government expenditure exceeds taxes) and thereby financial assets, and the initial flow of disposable income all on an equal scale. The national income increases by a multiplier process, reconciling the creation of government debt with the private sector's demand for net assets. But this increase in income raises the tax yield until it reaches the point of intersection with G' at the point Z'; a new stationary equilibrium will have been reached where the national income is at X'. During the transitional period the multiplier process must have ensured that government plus private debt has been created by an amount equal to $W' - W$, i.e. by exactly the amount which satisfied the equilibrium condition for desired private assets relative to disposable income.

Note particularly that although a norm for private-asset stocks is necessary for the model to have a solution at all, the equilibrium flow of income is determined by G and T alone. Had the asset norm schedule been different — had it for instance been as shown by the dotted line w, w' — the new solution for national income would equally have been at the point X' although the total amount of government debt created through the transitional period would have been less; it would only have been equal to $w' - w$.

We have thus reached the important conclusion that the national income flow, though it may be temporarily disturbed by monetary policy or random shocks, will in the long run be determined by fiscal stance alone. And characterization of the dynamic processes (which I have no time to discuss) will reveal that if marginal tax rates are high — say 0.4 to 0.6 as in most modern economies — the 'long run' in which fiscal policy rules income determination will only be a year or two.

INFLATION ACCOUNTANCY

What about Keynes' sidestepping of the problem of inflation by denominating output in terms of wage units? Here again a sensible discussion cannot proceed unless we start from a full and consistent set of accounts.

If we are to analyse the determination of real national income and expenditure flows we need to see how these are interrelated with stock variables also denominated in real terms. Consistency will require principles identical with those which apply to a nominal stock flow system. In particular the real income and real expenditure of every sector must be defined in such a way that any difference between the two flows is equal to the change in the real assets that sector owns less the change in its real debts.

This formal equivalence is not achieved, as simultaneous consideration of stocks and flows immediately reveals, if, in harmony with current practice, nominal income and nominal expenditure are simply deflated by a price index. The easiest way to convey the point is to imagine a period in which the nominal income of a sector is exactly equal to nominal expenditure while inflation is occurring. If income and expenditure were now both deflated by one price index they would obviously still be equal to one another, which appears to imply that net *real* stock of assets is constant. But this is clearly wrong. With nominal income and expenditure equal to one another it is the net nominal stock of financial assets which is constant; but then, since inflation is occurring, the real net stock of assets must be *falling*. So a consistent inflation accountancy requires not only that the nominal income flow is deflated, but that income is *in addition* adjusted downwards to allow for the erosion of the real value of the opening stock of (net) assets by inflation during the period.

The most important application of the principle of inflation accountancy is to the government's fiscal stance. The government's real income (taxes net of interest) must be defined in such a way that if it equals real public expenditure the real value of the national debt does not change. This condition will be satisfied (in accordance with the principles just set down) if the income flow is first deflated by a price index and then has added to it an amount representing the so-called inflation tax – the reduction in the real value of all government debt (including 'outside' money) because of inflation.

Now provided we can postulate (which seems uncontroversial) that the private sector norms are for real assets and liabilities relative to real income, then by an argument identical to that in the preceding main section the flow of real national income, expenditure and output will necessarily be governed by the real fiscal stance alone. This is a crude Keynesian conclusion with a vengeance: it makes fiscal policy rule the unemployment roost once again and is in no way conditional on there being sticky prices or wages, on expectations or anything else at all.

Yet there are three kinds of constraint which can, in reality, come into force. First there is a potential physical capacity constraint – something which we can ignore in 1983. Second there may be a balance-of-payments constraint if a country is not sufficiently competitive at home and abroad. Third there may be an inflation constraint in the sense that rising real output and employment generate high or, still worse, accelerating inflation requiring an ever-increasing nominal budget deficit to satisfy the condition that the real stock of financial assets expands fast enough. In the real world the expansion of the real fiscal stance must accordingly be considered to be the necessary but not sufficient condition for achieving sustained growth and full employment.

NOTES

1. In other words people thought and built econometric modesl which were based on an 'IS' mechanism without any (operative) 'LM' process; if these models contained a representation of the financial system, that did not make any important differences to the solutions they generated.
2. Taken from Moggridge, D. E. (1976) *Keynes*, London, Macmillan, 130.
3. Hicks, J. R. Mr Keynes and the Classics; a suggested interpretation, *Econometrica*, **5**.
4. In the *General Theory* it was the only driving force; neither the fiscal system nor foreign trade feature in Keynes' own theoretical model.
5. Christ, C. A. (1966) A shortrun aggregate demand model of the interdependence and effects of monetary and fiscal policies with Keynesian and Classical interest elasticities. *American Economic Review, Papers and Proceedings*, 1966.
   Ott, D. J. and Ott, A. F. (1965) Budget balance and equilibrium income, *Journal of Finance*, **20**, March.
6. Blinder, A. S. and Solow, R. M. (1973) Does fiscal policy matter? *Journal of Public Economics*, **2**, November.
7. Tobin, J. and Buiter, W. H. (1976) Long run effects of fiscal and monetary policy on aggregate demand. In J. L. Stein (ed) *Monetarism*, Amsterdam: North Holland.
8. 'Poverty in Plenty: Is the economic system self-adjusting?' A broadcast in 1934 cited by John Eatwell (1983) in *Whatever happened to Britain*, London: Duckworth.
9. This quotation and the one from Disraeli which follows are both taken from the historical section of Sir Ian Gilmour (1983) *Britain Can Work*, Oxford: Martin Robertson.
10. From *East Coker* by T. S. Eliot.
11. In the appendix I have attempted to set out rigorously, if briefly, why this is so, and how the confusion in Keynesian macroeconomics can be resolved and why the most important change which I have had to make in my views about macroeconomic policy has nothing to do with the theory of inflation as such, nor about monetary aggregates, 'crowding out' etc. It has to do with the importance of the proper inflation accounting of all national-income accounting concepts — i.e. stocks as well as flows. It is (maybe?) slowly coming to be realized that, to be meaningful as a measure of fiscal stance, a budget deficit must be corrected for cyclical movements. It has still to be understood that public deficits, if they are to be measures of the determinants of real demand and output, must also be corrected for the erosion of the money value of the stock of government debt (including 'inside' money) from inflation.
12. Since I gave this talk there has been a significant recovery in the United States. I regard this as confirmation of my views since it has been the

consequence of an expansionary fiscal policy (albeit adopted by default) and has occurred notwithstanding very high real interest rates.
13. Keynes, J. M. (1982) *Collected Writings*, Vol. XXVI. Edited by D. Moggridge, London: Macmillan, pp. 287 and 288.
14. Godley, W. and Cripps, F. (1983) *Macroeconomics*, Oxford: Oxford University Press.
15. Readers who find the following notes scanty or obscure may care to look at a fuller exposition of the same system of ideas in Cripps and Godley, op. cit., and Godley, W. (1983) Keynes and the management of real national income and expenditure, paper for the Keynes Centenary Conference, Cambridge, July 1983 (forthcoming, CUP).
16. Incidentally the whole development of national accountancy would also have been different, since these accounts have concentrated on flows almost to the exclusion of stocks.
17. I am going to confine my theoretical discussion to fiscal policy in a closed economy for reasons of space. It would, however, be fairly easy to expand the model to include foreign transactions. I also ignore here the possible implications of nominal capital gains.

5

Stagflation as an Issue of Economic Policy

ERIK LUNDBERG

INTRODUCTION

In this paper I concentrate my attention on the *stagflation issue* as the main basis of the fear of economic decline. I do it to a considerable extent from the point of view of a small economy like Sweden, where all of the relevant questions of stagflation have appeared quite clearly. Certain generalizations with regard to the world economy are also made.

I start from the macroeconomic problems as they have appeared in most industrialized countries during recent years. Then I turn my attention to policy issues as they appear and as they are dealt with by economists. The nature of stagflation is such that it often leads to crises of policy or policy dilemmas.

Sophisticated model building that is more or less independent of economic realty is pushed aside. Abstract model builders are apt to neglect or even forget economic reality. Instead, the *policy issues* as they have come up after 1973 are my main topic, issues determined by the stagflation of our economies, the imbalances caused by stagflation, and by the failures of actual policies.

ASPECTS OF THE STAGFLATION PROBLEM

So many problems since the middle of 1970s are common to nearly all industrial countries. As an introduction let me just name them:

1. Zero or very low rates of economic growth combined with much below-normal productivity rises.
2. High and rising unemployment.

3. Underutilization of production capacity.
4. Inflation rates higher than acceptable; inflation expectations built into the system.
5. Squeeze of profit rates, pessimistic profitability expectations.
6. Investment in industry and housing at relatively low levels.
7. High nominal and real interest rates.
8. Large government budget deficits.
9. Considerable deficits in the current balance of payments.
10. Structural crises connected with international excess capacity in certain key branches of industry: iron and steel, shipping and shipyards, petrochemical industry, aircraft industries, iron ore.
11. In varying degrees structural imbalances of a more general kind: too small an industrial sector (de-industrialization) and too large a public sector.

These various features of the stagflation crises are clearly interdependent. At this stage I just present them as they appear in the public debate.

Intermixed with these stagflation problems there are *policy crises* of similar kinds in all countries. Restrictive monetary policies introduced in the second half of the 1970s are being carried out under the leadership of the United States and British Governments and forced upon most other countries. Potential revivals from the cyclical recession have been checked — at least up to 1983 — and the stagflation problem preserved. Thus, a *policy dilemma* is manifest in all industrial countries; the target of bringing down the inflation rate is in conflict with the aim of increasing employment and getting the economy up on the highway of balanced growth.

A conflict in the working of fiscal and monetary policies is evident everywhere also, as big and rising budget deficits are disturbing the anti-inflation impact of a restrictive monetary policy, generating high and rising interest rates.

Structural problems — aggravated by stagnation — are raising issues of *industrial policy*, mostly strengthening protectionist attitudes. Over capacity in many and the same fields over the whole international community tends to create rising pressure for internal solutions by means of government subsidies in more or less refined forms. Restrictions of imports and subsidies of exports are creating rising disturbances to international trade. The efforts — especially of small, open economies — to attain export-led growth tends to be frustrated under conditions of stagnating world trade. There are signs of *competitive devaluations* as an alternative to competitive austerity.

This brings me to the *global aspects* of prevailing national imbalances. Slow and distorted growth of the volume of international trade is a consequence of internal stagnation and structural imbalances in the industrial world. The low levels of demand for raw materials and industrial products from the less-developed countries imply a number of imbalances to these countries: big balance-of-payments deficits, slowing down of production growth, high and rising underemployment.

Varying rates of inflation, exchange rates far out of equilibrium (over- and undershooting) and big unstable capital movements from surplus to deficit countries, all these are parts of the global disequilibria. The cumulative building up of tremendous international debts and claims belongs to the prevailing global instability. Fears of international financial collapse and the resulting restriction of credit supply to less-developed countries aggravate severely the stagnation tendencies of the world economy.

There are two specific features of the present phase that have to be kept in focus. First, the very size of the disruption of the national economics reckoned from 1973 stands out. Since the 1930s and the Second World War there has never been such great deviations from the normal path of development. Secondly, these deviations (gaps in relation to previous trends) create serious *disorientations* with respect to the current and future course of events among wage earners, consumers, enterprises as well as among governments as policy-makers. This means more fundamental *uncertainty* as to future earnings, prices, profits, interest rates, exchange rates etc. as well as to policy reactions by the authorities. *Pessimistic moods* as to the future tend to dominate the minds of investors; short-term financial operations of all kinds appear far more profitable than long-term productive investments. All this stands in glaring contrast to the balanced growth path of the previous 20–25 years when booms and recessions represented small deviations from steady trends.

GENERAL ISSUES AS TO THE POLICY FRAMEWORK

There is a kind of crisis also with regard to the *analytical interpretation* of the developments. This refers to the *policy debate* as well as to the choice of policy strategy and to the underlying theoretical type of policy framework. The wide dispersion in views as to choice of models and the fight between schools is characteristic of this time of crisis. I shall mention some of the main points of the debate without going deeply into the controversies.

The first question to be raised is simply: Has there been a fundamental change in the functioning of the economies? The very fact of the big deviation from earlier trends means that economists have no or little evidence of the behaviour of an economy in these 'outside' regions. One may think of the unusually high unemployment rates, the persistent and high inflation rates, the unusual size of the gap between full capacity output and actual production. The very length of the period of stagflation experience should create new behaviour patterns and new attitudes by households, trade unions and firms. The collapse of the Phillips relation is common experience to most economies.

Many economists stress issues pertaining to disturbances from *supply shocks* as distinct from the earlier more common demand changes. New types of disequilibria will appear when a downward shift in the production function (or in the terms of trade) occurs that may imply too high real wages, squeezes of profit margins and serious problems of adjustment. In spite of this, econometricians tend to maintain, and are even able to show, evidence that there was no significant disruption in the early 1970s; the system of econometric equations constructed on statistical experience before 1974 works about as well for the period thereafter. I am unconvinced. The issue will be discussed when analysing the Swedish case.

We can ask whether it is the *supply side* of the system that seems to be especially out of order. In a number of countries the retardation of the gross national product (GNP) growth rate and a significant decline of the rate of productivity rise has been observed for the period after 1973. The productivity retardation is very much discussed as a new phenomenon having important implications as to the working of the economies. We economists are most ignorant and weakest in our analysis when dealing with production capacity and supply restriction problems.

It is not difficult to understand in a general intuitive way how and why productivity growth has retarded significantly in all countries. A simple version of Verdoorn's law is useful here in which a close positive relation is observed between production and productivity growth rates. But low aggregate productivity growth is also a function of the stagnation in GNP growth, resulting from a low utilization of capacity, a low rate of investment and slower adjustment to structural imbalances of the capital stock combined with reduced mobility of labour.

Intuitively we may offer the following explanation. The supply constraints to economic growth have become more binding, with the 1972/73 boom of primary goods and the two oil-price shocks as significant evidence. As a result the *expectation* of new price explosions when the economy approaches boom conditions may work as a constraint not least via expected policy reactions.

The old notion of capacity growth and the measuring of the gap (the McCracken or Okun gap) from actual growth has become muddled with the recent loss of orientation. An expansion of effective demand and production tends to encounter supply constraints at an early stage of revival in the form of rising prices and wage costs. However, aggregates of demand and supply can never tell the whole story. It is on the micro level that the brakes occur.

Again the case is not clear. Demand and supply sides interact and we often do not know and can not know exactly how restrictions on growth come about. The stagflation phenomenon – this tragic combination of inflation, slow or no growth and underutilization of resources – is by many economists regarded exclusively as a result of failures of ambitious Keynesian stabilization policies: when unemployment is considered too high, expansive monetary and fiscal policies will cause a rise in demand and employment. But within a short time there will appear a new wave of wage inflation and in many cases also balance of payments disturbances, followed by new restrictive policies.

It is quite easy to picture the failures of *stabilization policies* in various countries during the period 1973–82; expansive policies that have not solved the employment and growth problems, followed by restrictive policies that have not succeeded in bringing down the inflation rate effectively. The lack of international coordination of policies is another type of failure.

One outstanding reaction to these experiences has led to experiments with monetary policy along the lines of fixed targets of money supply. Conflicts with fiscal policy, especially with regard to prevailing large budget deficits, have resulted in extremely high nominal and real interest rates since 1979. Spreading from the United States and British credit markets over the whole world, these high rates have deepened and prolonged the present international recession.

As economists we may react to the very unsatisfactory state of the economies by suggesting various kinds of *rational solutions*. But we differ as to emphasis on the various *aims*: desired rate of employment, inflation, growth, income distribution etc. That is unavoidable. Some of us put the main emphasis on the failure of the system to create full employment and use of resources, on the suffering caused by high unemployment rates, on the big losses of production. Other economists regard too high rates of inflation as the overwhelming issue, partly by being an indication of a fundamental disequilibrium and malfunctioning of the economy.

It is interesting to note that we as economists use very different models — both as to analysing effects of policy measures but also as means of persuasion in popular debate. The Keynesian, the monetarist, the new classical and rational hypothesis schools with many nuances are all still in existence, none completely rejected by an actual failure in application. Behind each type of model (or school of thought) there is some kind of ideology. Let me illustrate.

On the one side there is a strong underlying belief in the effective functioning of markets, including labour and capital markets, when free from government interference. There are potential equilibrium positions existing where the actual problems of misallocation of resources and of unemployment are quickly and effectively solved and conditions of balanced growth are satisfied. At the other extreme there are prevailing convictions about the fundamental instability properties of a market system, especially with reference to capital accumulation and to the labour market. Government interference and planning is needed for achieving the aims of stability and growth. A difference in fundamental *Weltanschauung* is behind these contrasting policy frame works.

Economists from the various schools are quite able to suggest rational improvements of current policies and alternative solutions to the stagflation dilemma. However, one problem with economists' advice has to do with the question of optimum degree of political naiveté. From the point of view of an abstract model, rational policy solutions can be deduced. But the distance from the actual world of politics is wide, and some of the assumptions in the model can be doubted or are not at all accepted. The political realities are not amenable to the advice of economists, however well based on economic theory. Economists are not good — except in abstract formulations — at including (endogenize) political response mechanisms in their system. They will always have to face the forbidding issue of what is politically realistic or what can be considered as politically possible in some 'long-run' sense. How far away from or ahead of political reality should an economist be?

From the point of view of the potential existence of rational policy solutions (in the economists' models) much of the present stagflation crisis may be regarded as part of a *political crisis* – national and international. Most Western governments are weak, dependent on uneasy coalitions. The pressures from groups with short-term views and interests are strong, confrontations of interest groups frequent and compromise solutions may even tend to aggravate the problems. There are conflicts of aims that have become more serious since the 1960s. New attitudes to work and environment have implied serious complications. All this means that the *general policy milieu* for the effective use of policy in most countries has deteriorated since the 1960s. I shall illustrate this type of complication with the case of Sweden. The collapse of the 'Swedish model' gives a good illustration of the general tendencies discussed in this section.

THE CASE OF SWEDEN – POLITICS AND POLICIES

General issues of the Swedish experience

Swedish developments and policies since the middle of the 1970s are of interest as an outstanding case of failure, in sharp contrast to the successes in stabilization policies and growth experience ever since the First World War. After 1974 the Swedish economy has shown more of stagnation and of imbalances of the kinds mentioned above than nearly all other industrial countries. The aims of Keynesian policies as well as of industrial and labour-market policies have been more ambitious than in other countries. But the only real achievement has been the unemployment rate, keeping it below 3.5 per cent during the stagflation period.

The lack of efficiency and consistency of the policies carried out by weak governments is a fact. Certainly the problems of stabilization and growth had become much greater and more complicated than ever before during the post-war period – but probably not more so than in other small economies. The main issue here refers to the political, institutional, psychological background of the unsuccessful policies. It is primarily the deterioration of the policy milieu that I shall try to clarify.

Up until the mid 1970s, whenever something called the Swedish model was the topic of international debate, politicians and economists consistently referred to Sweden in highly positive terms.[1] In a more narrow sense, the concept had primarily been applied to conditions on the Swedish labour market, reflected by the ability of employers' and employees' organizations to reach reasonable wage settlements, while under an obligation to keep labour disputes at a minimum. The parties were supposed to share a common social outlook regarding the value of free negotiations, exempt from government interference. This included a positive attitude towards the competitive conditions of a market engaged in free international trade, combined with acceptance — also by the Confederation of Trade Unions — of the necessity of sufficiently high profitability in private enterprises for guaranteeing investment large enough to expand production and increase productivity.

In a wider sense, the Swedish model embodied aspects of overall trends in society such as progressive social development, including high employment levels, continuous movement towards income equalization and rapid expansion of the social security system as well as the rest of the public sector. All this actually occurred during the decades between the end of the Second World War and the early 1970s. Sweden's GNP continued to rise (from a relatively high per capita level at the close of the war) at a fairly steady annual rate (of 4—5 per cent), while the rate of the general price level increase remained relatively low (3—4 per cent per year). Stabilization policy appeared to be successful and total unemployment varied between 1.5 and 3 per cent. No serious internal or external imbalances arose during this period.

The breakdown of the Swedish model

After 1973 the Swedish economy seems to have disintegrated. Labour disputes have become much more frequent; many regard the general strike and mass lockout in May 1980 as a conclusive signal that Sweden had reached the end of an epoch. During the 1970s, the average annual inflation rate rose to about 10 per cent and the average growth rate declined to 1—2 per cent per year. Wages 'exploded' between 1974 and 1976 in an inflationary wave that had not been parallelled since the Korean crisis. The recessions deepened, industrial production stagnated and the successful operation of earlier post-war stabilization policy disappeared.

A number of economic imbalances appeared in the mid 1970s: record balance of payments deficits, rapidly rising deficits in the government budget, structural crises in several industrial sectors accompanied by a substantial decline in investments in industry. Tendencies towards rising unemployment could be halted (or disguised) only through a highly expansive labour-market policy, including subsidies to the private sector and above all a rapid increase of employment in the public sector. Earlier notions of harmony as to how effectively the labour market, wage formation and the market system in general functioned in the interplay with the public sector and government policy have been replaced by apprehensions about continued high inflation, stagnation and severe conflicts between labour and capital, and between wage-earner groups.

THE EFO MODEL AND ITS DISINTEGRATION

Outline of the Model

A strategic part of the Swedish experiment referred to a consensus as to the guide lines of wage determination, the so called EFO-norm. This was based on a model of inflation in a small, open economy developed in the late 1960s by a group of economists from the main organizations of the labour market. It is indicative of the change in political climate that this EFO-consensus has more or less disappeared since the middle of 1970s.[2] The basic premise shared by the parties on the Swedish labour market — and by the governments — was the preservation of the competitiveness of Swedish industry in relation to foreign production — on the domestic as well as the export market. The equilibrium condition ultimately concerned the balance-of-payments. As exchange rates were pegged (according to the Bretton Woods system) up until the beginning of the 1970s, in the last analysis there was a clearly limited margin for wage increases in the sector most exposed to international competition. All of the parties were in agreement on this point — at least in principle. Of course, the labour unions could never explicitly proclaim the necessity of maintaining satisfactory profit margins as one of their goals. In collective bargaining it was always self-evident that the labour unions would try to squeeze out as much as possible. But, at least in the long run, employer opposition combined with the corrective effects of wage drift did produce results which more or less adhered to EFO-norm.

The crucial assumption of the EFO model is that the sectors of the economy that are directly exposed to foreign competition (the traded-goods sector) act as wage leaders. That implies that the average increase of wage costs in the traded-goods sector is determined by the degree of competitiveness of this sector. This means that in equilibrium growth the rise of wage costs will be equal to the sum of the rate of international price rise and the rate of growth of labour productivity. Under this condition the share of profits in value added will be kept constant. This rate of rise of wages is then transmitted to the rest of the economy, i.e. to the sheltered sectors. Here the rise of prices will be determined by the principles of cost-push and mark-up pricing. As the rate of productivity growth will be considerably lower than in the industrial sector exposed to international competition, the rise of prices in the sheltered sector will be larger than in the exposed sector, corresponding to the difference in average productivity change.

In the discussion of the model there has from the beginning been confusion about its *positive* versus its *normative* contents or interpretation. The model has been applied and tested empirically with regard to wage and price developments during the post-war period. Over longer periods – longer than the business cycle – the results seem quite satisfactory up to 1973.

The EFO-economists themselves wished to regard their model also as a 'long-run approach to wage policy' that could serve as basis and norm for wage policy of the labour market organizations. It would give 'a main course' of both actual and desired wage-cost development – with limited deviations from year to year. The self-correcting mechanism when actual wages in the short term were over- or undershooting the target was discussed in a rather crude way. The assumptions as to the working of this mechanism included endogeneous policy reactions of the government in booms and recessions under conditions of a fixed exchange rate. In fact, however, the model ultimately was based on assumptions of aggregate equilibrium conditions to which the economy was tending in the longer run – a notion that apparently is mixed with normative considerations. This type of mixing is in fact an old Swedish tradition with Knut Wicksell as a pioneer.

At this point I would like to refer to an important contribution by Franz Ettlin.[3] In his extended wage-determination model he has in fact formulated the short-run relationships that generate the longer-run 'main course'. The starting point is a generalized Walrasian price adjustment framework, when labour-market tensions appear both as excess supply of labour (corresponding to a 'true' unemployment rate) and excess demand for labour (over actual employment, a 'true' vacancy rate). It should be observed that these functions include the level of money wages as a variable. Ettlin stresses the point that the unemployment rate cannot and should not (as often in the case) be used as a proxy for the excess demand for labour. Demand for labour within the Walrasian framework is, according to the assumed production function, related to labour productivity and prices of output. The dynamization of the econometric system (with adequate time lags) gives a short-term determination of wage and price changes (of Phillips relation type) and in a longer-term approach gives approximately the EFO main course.

Ettlin maintains the dual structure of the EFO model in an exposed and a sheltered sector. But his results are based on adequate dynamic theory and careful identification of the equations. He can therefore give richer and more reliable results. His neoclassical type of short-run model yields long-term results that are close to the EFO main course development of price and wages. He is able to show that the partial effect of the unemployment rate on the rate of change of money wages is only of a transitory nature; in the longer run it is the wage *level* that is effected (implying a horizontal Phillips curve).

The extension and precision of the EFO model that is exemplified by Ettlin's work is needed for improved empirical verification and research. But as to the *norms* of wage and price development we have to use very simple guidelines. The EFO model could evidently be used as a long-term norm as long as certain strategic conditions were satisfied.

Unfortunately, the development of ideas supporting the norm of the model contained a germ that could cause the model to self destruct. Labour union economists advocated that profit margins should gradually be narrowed. They regarded this as an aim of wage policy. It would contribute to a structural transformation of the economy under the condition of generally restrictive monetary and fiscal policies which made it difficult for firms to compensate for increased costs under constant exchange rates. A squeeze from labour costs in conjunction with a solidaristic wage policy — with equal wage increases throughout regardless of individual firms' financial strength and productivity — would, in fact, bring about a general rise in productivity. This would occur along several paths. Firms would have to implement rationalization measures in order to cover cost increases at given internationally determined prices. The solidary cost squeeze would also force weak firms and subsectors to cut back or discontinue operations and thereby relinquish production resource to expanding and profitable firms and subsectors. The structural transformation precipitated by the labour-cost pressure would be — and actually became — an important cause of the rapid rise in industrial productivity (by some 7–8 per cent per year during the 1960s).

In this version of the EFO model the rise in productivity is not given; instead it is to some degree a function of the rate of increase in labour costs. The trade union economists argue in favour of such a tight squeeze on profit margins that employment problems arising in relatively weak subsectors had to be solved by selective government policies eventually by subsidy measures.

The Breakdown of the EFO Model

The inflationary international upswing, accentuated by the oil price shock in late 1973, was too great a disturbance for the efficient working of the EFO model. Labour-cost increases amounting to more than 60 per cent for the period 1974–6 were, from 1975, in fact led by the unions representing employees in the public sector. This was, without doubt, a striking departure from the EFO principle of the pacesetting status of the competitive sector. The ultimate result was such a large 'overshooting' in the development of wages that the Swedish economy was hit by a profound cost and profitability crisis. This not only caused Swedish export industry to loose many of its markets, but also intensified the structural crises which evolved during the 1970s.

The increase in labour costs was not accompanied by a rise in productivity as would have been normal according to the model. On previous occasions, a minor overshooting would subsequently be corrected by recession years with correspondingly subnormal wage increases. But this profitability and cost crisis could not be rectified easily under the conditions of a stagnating economy. The depreciations of the Swedish crown in 1977 and 1981 lagged behind and were apparently too small.

The efficient operation of the EFO model up until the beginning of the 1970s was implicitly based on the condition that targeted nominal wage increases would lead to a satisfactory rise in real wages — even after taxes. This relation was disrupted in the 1970s by the combination of an increase in the inflation rate and a steep rise in direct taxes. The marginal tax level — elevated by the inflation — widened the gap between wage increases before and after taxes. The 'conversion rate' for the average industrial worker from the later half of the 1970s was cut down to about 60 per cent, i.e. a nominal wage increase of 1 per cent did not yield more than a 0.6 per cent rise in income after taxes. In order for purchasing power of wages to remain unchanged when the consumer price index increased at the rate of 10 per cent, this relation implied that wages would have to rise by 17 per cent.[4] When the subsequent acceleration of expected price increases is also taken into account, wage demands would need to be at least 10 per cent higher.

A more primitive policy norm seems to have replaced the EFO model. It is based on the simple and correct notion that real wage costs in Sweden are too high and have to be brought down as a necessary condition of bringing the Swedish economy out of its disequilibrium. Instead of choosing the long uncertain road of depressing the economy, the governments have used the more traditional instrument of devaluation. The new social democratic government (from September 1982) started its mandate by a big bang devaluation of the Swedish crown by 16 per cent, thereby creating a clearly undervalued currency. It was made clear that this measure implied lower real wages (for 1983 by some 3–5 per cent) and higher profits. The target is to take unavoidable, one-time acceleration of inflation during 1983 and thereafter attain a stable pattern of development with no prospects of an early strong recovery of real wages. This unusual declaration of a socialist government was clearly related to the general crisis consciousness of the Swedish people in all circles that had not existed in the 1970s. But the success of the devaluation policy is unfortunately determined by a number of policy-related conditions inside and outside the country.

UNCERTAIN PROSPECTS – THE POLITICAL CONSTRAINTS

The extended welfare state and stagnation

The combination of the excessively high rate of labour-cost

increases after 1973 and the structural imbalances that development in the branches of industry exposed to international competition has meant that the 1974 peak in the volume of industrial production was not reached even in 1982. An undersized industrial sector and an oversized public sector are essential components of the fundamental disequilibrium in the Swedish economy. This is revealed by the combination of a balance-of-payments deficit (corresponding to 3–4 per cent of GNP) and a financial crisis of the government with a budget deficit amounting to more than 12 per cent of GNP.

The Swedish Long-Term Planning Commission Reports (of 1980 and 1981) estimated that, under reasonable assumptions about the elimination of imbalances during the 1980s, there will have to be a gradual, slow decline in the real standard per employed person. There will always be a great risk that the contention between groups for increases in income *in a zero-sum game* will intensify inflationary strains. The objective of further income and wage equalization, which is usually regarded as an essential issue especially during periods of economic stagnation, clashes with the needs of providing incentives that are strong enough to stimulate an increase in work and investments. Arguments in favour of keeping high profitability, reduced progressiveness of direct taxes, improved relative wages for skilled workers and in the industrial sector are incompatible with existing egalitarian norms in Sweden.

A kind of *socio-psychological transformation of climate* has taken place which incorporated both political and economic dimensions. The very success of the Swedish model during the 1950s and 1960s seems to have triggered off counteracting forces which have impaired its efficiency and credibility. This means that the root of this transformation lie back in time, perhaps a decade before the manifestation of crisis.

Rapid and steady economic growth throughout a quarter of a century tended to create attitudes whereby such expansion was conceived of as self-evident and inexorable. It was taken for granted and, in effect, became an integral part of prevailing social mechanisms. Problems related to the rapid growth of the public sector and policies of income equilization seemed affordable and caused a minimum of economic disturbance as long as this growth appeared to be self-perpetuating.

An uninterrupted rise in the level of GNP resources led to attitude changes and new demands. Since the mid 1960s the original and simple economic policy goals (full employment, stable prices and rapid growth) have been reoriented towards more ambitious welfare aims. Price stabilization has been relinquished as an objective when other goals were given priority. Security and equity aims have taken precedence at the same time as welfare costs associated with high productivity and effective resource allocation, have been regarded as increasingly serious. One example is the intense reaction to the high labour mobility which prevailed during the decades of rapid growth. Labour legislation during the 1970s reflects demands for job security at the place of work or in the region, in place of the general government pledge of full employment in the economy as a whole.

The enormous increase in the total expenditures of the public sector (including transfers) — which corresponded to 25 per cent of GNP in 1950 and about 70 per cent during the beginning of the 1980s — is the outcome of political decision-making under expectations of permanent rapid economic expansion. The result is not only an expression of high income elasticities as to public services (at zero prices). Efforts to achieve a more equalized distribution of income and wealth play an important role. This is evidenced by great efforts to improve the position of low-income groups and pensioners at the same time as the progressiveness of income taxes has been rising radically. Leading circles of politicians and the organizational bureaucracy have grown much-less inclined to accept the level of corporate profitability ruling during the 1960s — being an important source of the uneven distribution of income and wealth. It may be asserted, to quote Assar Lindbeck, that 'Swedish politicians seem to think Sweden is so rich that the Swedes can even afford to consume the prerequisites for the existing welfare'.

What to do about stagnation?

The Swedish economy suffers from imbalances which may be interpreted as stemming from insufficient access to productive resources and fears that GNP growth during the 1980s will be too slow. There seems to be a kind of *political and social schizophrenia*, i.e. of distorted attitudes both within individuals themselves and between different groups of people. On the one hand Sweden has achieved such a large total supply of resources (GNP per capita) that there is plenty of — and perhaps even more than enough — room for high levels of welfare and quality of life, as long as given resources are utilized and distributed in a reasonable way. This is a plea for solidarity. On the other hand prevailing serious imbalances of the economy and the threat of potential conflicts of interest imply that now, more than ever, an increase in GNP is a necessary prerequisite for arriving at a harmonious solution to imminent economic problems. The Swedish model was based on simple rationality and optimistic outlooks for the future — which no longer seem to exist. The new schizophrenic attitudes are seriously influenced by *genuine uncertainty* about future prospects.

Dilemmas such as these could possibly be resolvable if politicians, trade union representatives etc. were convinced that stronger incentives, which did create a number of temporary injustices or reinforce old ones, would have a quick, positive effect on growth, productivity and the balance-of-payments. Confidence in the effectiveness of the market system is the real issue at stake. Experience during the 1950s and 1960s has shown that such confidence used to exist; it was one of the conditions underlying the effective operation of the Swedish model. Today, however, attitudes and opinions are widely divergent and reflect the polarization of party politics. Critics in the socialist camp claim that larger profits, higher remuneration for certain kinds of work and risk-taking only serve to increase income and wealth of the well-to-do and fuel inflation. Solutions should instead be sought — avoiding big increases of profits — by various forms of collective savings put into wage-earners' and structural funds, combined with centralized investment planning — that is, by *drastic changes in the economic system*.

The social democrats seem to be convinced that in the longer run the present system must be changed in important respects. The main attention is devoted to the deficiency and instability of capital formation. The speculative shortsightedness of the financial system is one side of the issue. The combination of inflation and high tax rates has contributed to the result that short-term financial operation and real-estate transactions are so much more profitable than long-term investments in a new industrial capacity. As a result, industrial investments have been at much too low a level since 1976. Only rationalization (robotization) investments, by substitution of capital for labour, tend to pay off sufficiently well. The conclusion — similar to that of Keynes' in the *General Theory* — is the need for some kind of 'socialization' of the bulk of private capital formation.

One solution will be found in a combination of 'fund socialism' for the creation of a steady flow of risk capital and government-sponsored, long-term investments in new capacity (joint ventures) especially within industry and energy production. The social democrats as well as the central trade union organizations have in their programme the successive transfer of stock-ownership to collective funds, created by profit sharing and taxes on wage and salary payments. Under these conditions – it is maintained – high profitability and big profit incomes would – according to the socialist gospel – be much more easily tolerated than in a pure market system and could, therefore, be the basis of wage-stabilization programmes. An even more fundamental issue of fund socialism concerns the introduction of economic democracy by means of a rising share of collective ownership.

In this way the Swedish policy scene has been complicated by the provocation of a *system crisis*. This is not the place to present and discuss the various eventual future alternatives of a Swedish system of fund socialism. The policy complication refers to the extra uncertainty of the future that has been created in the business community, an increased lack of confidence that is affecting the entrepreneurial climate and, therefore, long-term private investment. In a way the French method of 'instant socialization' when Mitterrand came to power would seem much less ominous as to the working of the economy than the Swedish method of socialization (or collectivization), a process drawn out over a decade or more. This type of socialist reaction to the crisis of the mixed economy (of the Swedish model) is about as 'logical' as the opposite reaction of the monetarist or neoclassical camp arguing for restoring the conditions of a perfect market economy.

THE ARGUMENTS OF AN ECONOMIST FOR GROWTH

The supply side in recovery

In Sweden – as in a number of other countries – there are strong voices against taking continued growth as a policy target, instead such aims as the quality of life, small-scale production, etc. are stressed. This attitude also fails to understand the political realities. As economists we can give good reasons for the needs of continuous increase in the supplies of goods and services, for solving employment and poverty problems at home and abroad, for minimizing frictions when dealing with aims of improved equity.

The question is 'only' if and how an acceptable rate of growth (of at least 2–3 per cent per year) can be achieved. The potentials as to supplies of human skills, technical knowledge and capital exist as shown in several investigations of long-term development possibilities. One necessary condition — when looking at the supply side of the balance in a country like Sweden — refers to the need of a radical improvement of the *incentive system*: acceptance of reasonably high profitability in the private sector, reducing the progressiveness of direct taxes (at present varying between 60 and 85 per cent for the majority of employees) more wage differentiation between skilled and unskilled workers, etc. Economists are able to point to the relatively modest effects on income distribution of such measures, using persuasive arguments as to gains in productivity to be used for improving the standard of the lowest income groups. When pleading for an improved incentive system economists in Sweden are, however, likely to be advocating the politically impossible. We have to confront strong dogmatic arguments for more income and wealth equalization; the dynamics of egalitarian targets is such that the more equalization that is attained, the more excitement there exists about differences that still exist.

As economists we cannot prove by how much and when productivity augments as a result of a better incentive system. There are no reliable supply-side models. There is another important aspect that should be made explicit: the entrepreneurial activity connected with the 'creative destruction' process *à la* Schumpeter. The attention to the severe structural imbalances of the Swedish as of other countries' economies during the 1970s has been concentrated mainly on the destruction sides. Sick industries have been supported by governments on a large scale in Sweden. The creation side has been neglected. One explanation refers to the deteriorated 'entrepreneurial climate', to the tax system, to the uncertain and pessimistic state of expectations and also to future government policies. This factor is especially relevant in Sweden with regard to the fears as to the introduction of rapidly expanding collective ownership ('fund socialism'). As economists we are pleading for a more positive and creative climate of entrepreneuship and are from this point of view warning against a shift of the system of ownership.

The demand side in recovery

Bringing about a more flexible supply side with increased growth potential is, of course, only half the problem. Sufficient effective *demand pressure* is the necessary concomitant. Increased elasticity of supply and mobility of resources should imply a reduction and postponement of inflation during a growth revival.

Another strategic condition for a successful expansionary policy is that the price signals are correct, corresponding to the adjustment needs of the economy. From this point of view the large crown depreciation was needed. The higher export and import prices should signal and make profitable the redirection of production resources from private and public consumption to industry in the competitive sector. The aim is, of course, to attain an expansion process led by production for export and for import substitution. The government is preparing a moderate investment expansion programme as a stimulus to the economy, both from the demand and supply sides.

Can the Swedish experiment succeed again?

Two main question marks pertaining to the eventual success of Sweden's effort to break away from the international stagnation stand out. The first one refers to inflation. For how long a period will the crown be undervalued? There are lots of examples of unsuccessful devaluations due to a rapid response of internal inflation. The other question mark refers to the responses of the international economy, stagnating or expanding.

At some point on the way to 'full' employment and high utilization of resources, supply bottle necks and wage drift will aggravate the inflation issue. It is common and easy for economists to appeal to incomes policies and wage-freeze agreements. It is probably not enough that a socialist government has a 'working arrangement' with the trade union organizations. Such agreements have so far never worked satisfactorily over a period of more than 2 years.

A recurrent question arises. If and to what extent the government should carry out an accommodating policy when wage inflation has started? There is a hard lesson about the frustrating results of maintaining more or less full employment independently of the rate of wage and price increases. In the pre-1970s days of the Swedish experiment, the discipline came from the balance of payments and the fixed-exchange-rate policy. In a small open economy the space for independent policy is limited. After 1976 the exchange-rate policy has been clearly accommodating and the long-run results have been very inflationary.

All this means that after the 'one-time, inflation-devaluation wave' of 1982/83, the Swedish economy should and will try to return to a revised Swedish experiment of high employment development and a low rate of inflation. This is, anyhow, the long-run plan of the government. As the discussion above concerning the equilibrium conditions of the economy reveals, there will be severe political as well as economic obstacles in the way. There is one reason for optimism about a positive outcome and it is fundamental: the general concensus as to the main causes of the frustrating experiences of the period 1974–82. The same kinds of mistakes will not be repeated. New ones will certainly be made. But there is in my view a good chance of returning to a period of expansion. But clearly this possibility will be strongly conditioned by the international development if and when the world stagflation problems will be solved.

OVERCOMING THE INTERNATIONAL STAGFLATION

Coordinated aggregate demand policies

This long exposé of Sweden's policy problems in a stagflation economy is made on the understanding that these problems are more or less typical, that they exist in various degrees of severity in all industrial economies or are, at least, potentially there. Certainly other countries have tried other policy experiments and have often been more successful than Sweden. But the failures with regard to the restrictive policies from 1980 have been about the same. It is the sum of all the national restrictive policies that gives the world stagflation – at the same time as international depressive forces work back on the national economies.

There is some confirmed experience that the competitive sector of the Swedish economy can be expanding at high speed even when world trade is stagnating and exposed to protectionism, as was the experience in the 1930s. This experience cannot be easily repeated. Although the present depression is far less deep (however measured), the restrictive-policy attitudes seem to be much more consistent and therefore dangerous. As to Sweden we have also learned that after losing foreign markets the regaining of markets is not a symmetrical process.

Anyhow a strategy of export expansion and import substitution for small open economies is certainly not a general solution of world stagflation. Devaluation or austerity policies of these countries do not contribute to the revival of the world economy. The conclusion is that we need the locomotive roles of strong and large economies like the United States, West Germany and Japan. Economists are right in pleading for coordination of policies and must continue to do so against the background of rising dangers of nationalism and isolation.

The OPEC problem

It is illuminating in the consideration of policy alternatives to compare the developments after the first and the second oil-price shock. The shocks were of about the same order of size (corresponding to about 2 per cent of OECD GNP). From a naive Keynesian point of view the first period 1974–9 was a relative success and the second period after 1979 a conspicuous failure. But I maintain this view with some important reservations.

In a rough outline the recession of 1974–5 and the following revival and growth basically had quite normal features. There was an excessive international boom 1972–4 followed by a quick but relatively deep recession. The break of the boom was provoked by strong restrictive monetary policies, quite well coordinated over the OECD community. This was then followed – as in the normal business cycle pattern – by quite expansive fiscal and monetary policies, led by the United States from about the spring of 1975. In many countries the real interest rates fell close to zero or negative. A quick and strong revival followed with real GNP jumping up 1975/76 at a 5–6 per cent rate. And then came a continued steady, although relatively slow, growth that was interrupted by the combination of the new oil shock and sharp restrictive policies 1979/80.

It is worth observing that the policies up to 1978 were accompanied by a general retardation of the inflation rate and by an approach to general equilibrium in the balance of payments (the OPEC surplus had been effectively reduced up to 1978). This was also the triumph of recycling the OPEC dollars to cover most of balance-of-payments deficits of less-developed countries (without oil). This meant that the growth rates of these countries could be kept up around the 5 per cent range and that the growth rate of their import volume from the industrial countries was kept up. There was therefore expanding world trade around 5–6 per cent during this period.

The contrast with the years following the 1979 oil-price shock is appalling and need not be spelled out in this connection. In fact the protagonists of monetarist and new classical schools consider the period 1975–9 as an outstanding failure of Keynesian accommodating policies. They feel that expansive policies have just concealed and covered up all the postponed imbalances: of too high real wages, too low interest rates, of underlying balance of payments disequilibria. In fact, they argue, the Keynesian policies of accommodation aggravated the imbalances and made the task of the later restrictive policies still more urgent and difficult. Stagnation and depressive tendencies following the monetarist policies from 1979 are according to these economists, considered as necessary conditions for attaining equilibrium. The only thing surprising about these policies is the long period and the high real costs in unemployment and lost production needed before they can begin to work.

This controversy both as to the interpretation of actual developments and as to adequate government policies is ultimately based on contrasting ideologies. According to my own view – and ideology – the Keynesian type of policies of the 70s could have continued being successful if the new oil-price shock had not occurred. But certainly these policies would have had to be considerably modified and more restrictive with regard to the boom of 1979. And clearly the tremendous rate of credit expansion to less-developed countries could not continue.

The Brandt commission once emphasized the necessity of globalization of expansionary policies. The background is a tremendous waste of resources on a global scale, in the form of high unemployment and general under utilization of capacity. This is the overwhelming impression – bottle necks and inflation impulses should be regarded as passing incidents of constraint. There is thus according to this view place for revival of Keynesian attitudes both on a global and a national scale.

CONCLUDING REMARKS

Underlaying the failing stabilization and growth issues I have discussed is the deficient working of the political system, nationally as well as on the international level. There is a crisis of the democratic systems – not structured to solve big economic problems related to a world crisis. All over there are weak governments based on small or no majorities, looking for tactics to use before elections.

The economist can argue himself blue in the face about more adequate economic policies. The tragedy is that businessmen, trade union leaders, politicians do not live in the peaceful, rational world of the economists. The politicians are mostly nearsighted — looking forward to the next election. They earn votes not on high principles but by means of promises about government expenditures, selective policies, subsidies to regions etc. Economists have been trying to understand and incorporate these reactions. But they will never succeed in foreseeing the abrupt changes in policy strategies as in 1979/80 or — as I hope — in 1983.

This paper has concentrated on the policy dilemmas arising out of stagflation as they have appeared from the 1970s. I have tried to show the various characteristics and how and why stabilization and structural policies have failed. By way of illustration I have directed attention to the case of Sweden as rather typical of how and why policies tend to fail in a much more systematic way than in earlier periods.

Economists are quite able to explain the stagflation situation. Alternative models are helpful and complementary. We think that we also can present rational solutions, relying on simplified policy models. My purpose has been to discuss the narrow political restrictions on a rational policy, how conflicting aims and short-term views on political possibilities make a rational choice of adequate measures impossible. Again illustrations have been taken from Sweden where confusion of targets and the deficiency of political decision-making for adequate longer-term strategies seem to be outstanding. The interdependence of stagflating economics in the world make the problems still harder to solve.

It is easy to visualize a continuation and a deepening of the world's stagflation tendencies over the 1980s. In the industrialized world the revivals would be relatively short, never approaching high employment levels of earlier booms. The interruptions would come from new oil-price shocks, provoked by rising demand, or other supply restrictions. Repressive monetary policies by leading countries would follow accelerated inflation rates. Structural imbalances would be preserved and new ones added because of no or slow growth, accompanied by rising protectionism in many forms. The global financial vulnerability would add to the genuine uncertainty of the future course of inflation, exchange rates and markets. All this means typical low-level imagination as to new possibilities, basing forecasts on experiences of the early 1980s.

I prefer to visualize the trends in the 1980s in a more hopeful although perhaps less scientific way. As an old Keynesian economist (brought up in the Stockholm School) I am an optimist since we learn from mistakes, politicians as well as economists. I look forward to the realization of the clear failure of long-term restrictive monetary policies in the leading countries, not denying their short-term effectiveness in reducing inflation. The present strong revival in the United States gives revised policy attitudes based on expansive long-term policies under some coordination as between countries a chance. We have actually learned a lot from the stagflation experiences and are generally alarmed about the social and political consequences. Even in the welfare state of Sweden significant changes of attitudes are occurring, e.g. as to government expenditures and income taxes. There are in all countries rising reactions against the high interest rates and most important against the high and rising unemployment rates. As inflation rates have been brought down effectively, reduction of unemployment will get highest priority.

There is a rising understanding that the structural imbalances of the world economy can be solved effectively only under conditions of expanding production and trade. The constraints on growth from the supply side that will appear should not be solved by means of restrictive policies, but by means of active investments in the short-supply areas, including large global schemes of investment – complementing such projects on a national scale – for a stimulus on the world economy.

It is unemployment and an intolerable degree of underutilization of resources that is the main evil of stagflation. After so many years of stagflation and with the menacing prospects of a world crisis the political milieu will be open to radical changes of policy strategy in the direction of stimulus to the economies and accommodation of a lasting revival. That is my wishful hope and forecast, supported by some signs of policy revision in the United States.

The revival and expansion experiences during the recent period of 1975–9 seem to demonstrate effectively the inherent possibilities of balanced growth – within the industrial countries as well as on a global scale – when there is a minimum of restrictive policies in leading countries. There should be the same potential possibilities in the OECD-area reappearing after the current recession and stagnation. The inflation risk should be less than after 1975. The big difference refers to the vulnerable debt positions of so many less-developed countries. But one necessary condition for successive solution of the depressive and protectionist effects of the debt-service problem is a new, long enough period of expansion of the markets in industrial countries.

Economic growth will, of course, never again attain the record levels of the 1960s. But for the industrial world growth of around the good old 3 per cent on average per annum should be attainable and realistic. How much unemployment and inflation will accompany this rate of growth is anybody's guess. It will very much depend on what happens in the revival process of the various countries, when expectations of future inflation are formed, partly depending on how much of the budget deficits of the government will disappear with the return of economic growth. Also in the respect of stabilization policy we have learned a lot during passed years and should — in leading countries — be able to find good synthesises of Keynesian and monetarist settings.

My attitude as to the end of world stagflation is based on a motto from Confucius: 'It is better to light even a small candle rather than damn the darkness.'

NOTES

1. The expression 'the Swedish model' started to be used at the end of the 1930s. The concept is necessarily vague, having several dimensions and changing over time. It is generally used as an appreciation of the success of Swedish economic policy. A forthcoming article of mine in the *Journal of Economic Literature* gives a fuller explanation.
2. The letters EFO refer to the names of three economists — Edgren, Faxen and Odner — from the Swedish organizations representing labour and employers, who worked out the joint report of the workings of the wage system. The model is also referred to as the 'Scandinavian model' and 'Aukurst model'.
3. *Wage determination in the step quarterly econometric model of Sweden.* Presented at the Eleventh Annual World Meeting of Project Link, Helsinki, August, 1979.
4. The expression $(1 - t_m)/(1 - t_a)$ is the 'conversion rate' and is in this case equal to 0.6 where t_a is the average direct tax rate and t_m is the marginal tax rate. The inverse of this expression equals 1.7 and is the tax—wage multiplier, a concept introduced by me in *Business Cycles and Economic Policy*, London, 1957.

6

The Phyrric Victory – Unemployment, Inflation and Macroeconomic Policy

LARS OSBERG

At the Battle of Asculum in 279 BC, Greek mercenaries under the command of Pyrrhus, King of Epirus, defeated the Roman army, but at a cost in casualities which is supposed to have prompted Pyrruhus to say: 'Another such victory over the Romans and we are undone.' Pyrrhus himself was not among the casualties and survived through several more campaigns. The phrase 'Pyrrhic Victory' has passed into the language as a metaphor for an ill-conceived venture but, as the *Encyclopedia Americana* puts it: 'Although his conquests were temporary and he exhausted the resources of Epirus in his wars, Pyrrhus was considered in antiquity as one of the greatest generals of Hellenistic times.'

The parallel with modern-day macroeconomic policy is too apt to be resisted. The generals of the modern Western economies embarked, in the late 1970s, on a campaign against inflation and, like Pyrrhus, it must be conceded that by 1982 they had won an important victory – inflation was down to single digits in North America, Britain and many nations of Western Europe. However, the casualties from this campaign, in the shape of over 32 million unemployed in the OECD nations, have been far higher than were anticipated and there is little current anticipation for their early recovery. Like Pyrrhus, the decision-makers of this modern economic war will themselves survive but unlike Pyrrhus they are surrounded by a public who will not be satisfied with tales of noble victories in far off lands. The electorate of modern-day economies will want to know: why did we embark on this campaign in the first place? Why were the costs of the war against inflation so grossly underestimated? What are the future consequences of the current 'victory'? What analysis, and what strategy, will save us from similar 'victories' in the future?

This paper will argue that it was a concern with distributional issues, and not with economic efficiency, that started the war against inflation in the first place. It will argue that the distributional implications, and the aggregate costs, of this war were substantially mis-estimated and that this mis-estimate was, in large measure, due to the reintepretation of labour-market data, and especially of unemployment, which developed as part of the 'new labour economics' of the 1960s and 1970s. Since the perceived costs of unemployment shrank relative to the perceived costs of inflation, it is not surprising that the policy-makers shifted their attention to the control of inflation rather than the alleviation of unemployment. However, the achievement of a low inflation rate, at the cost of a prolonged period of high unemployment, does not simply return the economy to its situation prior to the acceleration of inflation. This period of high unemployment will necessarily alter the institutional structure of the labour market and create problems whose impact will be exacerbated by the other structural changes now being experienced by Western soceities. These issues are treated in the following three sections, while the conclusion discusses the avoidance of further similar 'victory'.

EQUITY ISSUES

In assessing why the decision was made to emphasize anti-inflationary policies in the later 1970s one must assess, to some degree, the motives of economic decision-makers. However, these motives are not open to public inspection and must be imputed from public pronouncements and from the observation of the foreseeable consequences of their decisions. Since one foreseable consequence of high unemployment is to weaken the bargaining power of trade unions and since another foreseeable consequence has been increased poverty and lower family incomes within the working class of the OECD nations, one explanation of deflationary policies is to see them as stark evidence of an attempt by national capitalist classes to impose discipline upon their respective proletariats (perhaps because these proletariats had become increasingly demanding, e.g. in 1968 in Europe). Although such analysis may explain the attitudes of some of the economic decision-makers of the OECD nations, to my mind it certainly cannot explain the motives of all decision-makers. Such analysis cannot explain why deflationary policies were able to gain widespread support, both among the general public (initially) and in academic and professional circles whose self interest was in no reasonable way advanced by deflation. One must admit that many people were convinced *by argument* of the evils of inflation and, in particular, of the inequities of inflation.

Arguments as to distributional equity are central to the discussion of whether one should adopt an anti-inflationary policy stance since it is very hard to argue reasonably for the choice of an anti-inflationary emphasis on pure efficiency grounds. An efficiency criterion would argue that one should compare the aggregate cost of a given degree of anticipated inflation or of a temporary recession to decrease inflation and inflationary expectations, and adopt the alternative which costs less. However, as Tobin (1972: 15) put it: 'According to economic theory, the ultimate social cost of anticipated inflation is the wasteful use of resources to economize holdings of currency and other non-interest bearing means of payment.' Nordhaus's (1973) estimate was that, in the United States, the cost of a 1 per cent increase in the rate of fully anticipated inflation (via the loss of consumer surplus due to the minimization of money balances) was, in 1962, of the order of 30 cents per capita per year – in 1980 dollars (assuming this loss of consumer surplus increased proportionally to family money income 1962–1980) this would amount to a cost to the United States economy of roughly $229 million per 1 per cent of anticipated inflation. By contrast Okun's (1978) estimate of the cost in foregone output of a recession sufficient to shave 1 per cent from the inflation rate was 10 per cent of a year's gross national product (GNP) – some $262 billion in 1980. Gordon's (1982) estimate is lower, some $152 billion, but either estimate of recessionary costs is an order of magnitude greater than the present value of the anticipated benefits of lower inflation. Only with very odd assumptions about the future cost of inflation (for example see Feldstein, 1979) is it possible to conclude that the losses in aggregate output of a given degree of anticipated inflation exceed the losses in foregone output of the recession which would be necessary in order to decrease inflation and inflationary expectations.

But of course the war on inflation was not founded on such comparisons. Rather the inflation fighters saw a given degree of inflation as possibly leading to accelerating inflation and emphasized the redistribution involved in unanticipated changes in the price level and in individual prices. Of course, unanticipated inflation, if it is truly unanticipated, does not change economic decisions *ex-ante* and cannot produce an *ex-ante* loss in economic efficiency. It is only after the fact of an unanticipated inflation that unanticipated redistribution of social product occurs. Unanticipated changes in the general price level, or accentuated variability in individual prices around anticipated changes in the general price level, impose on all market participants a sort of involuntary lottery. It is the inequities, i.e. the unanticipated redistributions, involved in such a lottery that have provided an indirect argument for an anti-inflation strategy on efficiency grounds. Okun (1981) has argued that the inequities and uncertainties of inflation impair the functioning of an economy which depends heavily on implicit contracts while Laidler and Rowe (1980) contend that confidence in the market economy itself will be undermined by continued inflation. At times these arguments are couched in mystical, if emphatic, language: 'It is surely now beyond dispute that one of the prime requirements for good economic performance over time in a market economy is a money that can be trusted' (Bouey, 1982).

However, it is now also surely 'beyond dispute', if controls are ruled out, that we cannot use deflationary policies to decrease inflation without also causing large-scale and prolonged unemployment. Hence the real issue is the comparison of inequities. We must compare the extent of the inequities involved in unanticipated inflationary redistribution of real output to the extent of the inequities involved when the unemployed are made to pay for the devotion which the rest of society feels for a stable price level. If we perceive the economy as composed of representative persons who may, occasionally, be unemployed as a result of their search behaviour between jobs, we will see the burden of unemployment as being fairly evenly spread throughout society and its inequities as being 'small' in comparison with the inequities of the involuntary lottery of inflation. However, if we perceive the labour market as composed of dissimilar individuals and groups we are more likely to perceive unemployment as partially involuntary, as concentrated in identifiable segments of the labour market, and as creating inequities which may be 'large' relative to the inequities created by inflation.

Analysis of the nature of modern labour markets is thus central both to the relative evaluation which one might place on inflation and on unemployment and it is also central to one's understanding of the causes of both of these phenomena. Unemployment is clearly a phenomenon of the labour market. Price inflation, unless one appeals to arguments based on ever-expanding mark-ups of prices over unit labour costs, is directly dependent on wage inflation, also a labour-market phenomenon. Why economic decision-makers in the late 1970s chose to emphasize inflation as the primary problem and why they chose the particular strategies which they used in therefore closely linked to their understanding of the functioning of labour markets, and to the evolution of a 'new labour economics' during the 1960s and 1970s.

'THE NEW LABOUR ECONOMICS'

During the early 1960s, labour economics still bore a good deal of the imprint of the work of the institutional writers of the 1950s (e.g. Kerr, 1950; Reynolds 1951). Best-selling texts (e.g. Woods and Ostry, 1962) were somewhat sceptical about the perfection of labour markets and tended to emphasize heavily the institutions of collective bargaining and labour relations, historical trends in labour-force growth and employment and the pattern of inter-occupational and inter-industry wage structure. It was normal to draw distinctions between types of unemployment and to prescribe different sorts of policy interventions to deal with each. Since this was, among other things, the initial period of computer development, there was a great concern with the extent of 'structural' unemployment — 'activist' manpower policies involving retraining programmes, relocation grants and increased subsidies to education were widely supported. 'Frictional' unemployment was briefly described as the unemployment of those who were 'between jobs'. Together with 'seasonal' unemployment it was seen as creating a minimum level of unemployment even at 'full employment' but in general it did not receive a great deal of attention. 'Cyclical' unemployment was seen as arising from insufficient aggregate demand — its prevention was the major focus of macro-economic stabilization policy. Perhaps partly because of lingering memories of the Great Depression, unemployment was, with the minor exception of 'frictional' unemployment, seen as largely involuntary, as concentrated in particular occupations and regions and as having, particularly for the long-term unemployed, extremely bad social implications. It was not uncommon to read such statements as 'unemployment is the worst scourge of a free enterprise system' (Woods and Ostry, 1962: 358).

However, one characteristic of mainstream labour economics during the 1960s and 1970s was a gradual process of 'de-institutionalization'. During the early 1960s the 'human capital revolution' rephrased the historic problem of explaining why workers have different jobs with different skills and receive different rates of pay into the problem of the optimal acquisition and depreciation of human capital over the life cycle. The analysis of qualitative differences in kind and types of skills (and the consequent rigidity and segmentation of the labour market) which had been so important to the institutional tradition fell out of fashion and was replaced by the discussion of differences in the quantity of 'human capital' possessed by individuals. Rather than emphasizing the detailed examination of particular employment relationships, labour economics changed its focus and became much more closely a form of applied microeconomics. Since problems which emphasized individual maximization of exogenously given independent preferences proved far more tractable than problems involving collective action, interdependent utilities or notions of 'fairness', the former sorts of problems received the majority of attention. Increasingly, labour economists left the messy institutional details of wage contours and collective bargaining to specialists in 'industrial relations' and concerned themselves with the testing of models of individual maximizing behaviour using quantitative data from secondary sources.

When Phelp's (1970) *Microeconomic Foundations of Employment and Inflation Theory* appeared, it therefore met a receptive audience. Indeed Phelps volume and the Friedman article of 1968 are landmark references to the study of the 'new unemployment' and the 'new macroeconomics' which influenced much of the 1970s. Viewing unemployment as search behaviour provided a theoretically elegant solution to an old criticism of decentralized market economies (i.e. unemployment). It received empirical support in the new emphasis placed on the large flows into and out of labour-force participation and employment in modern economies and the short duration of both the 'average' spell of unemployment and 'average' spell of employment (1.4 to 2.2 months and 20.8 months respectively in the United States during the early 1970s – Clark and Summers, 1979). When framed in terms of the 'representative man', search models implied that the incidence of unemployment is largely random, hence a decision not to stimulate the economy and to allow unemployment to rise is equitable in the same sense that a lottery where all individuals have the same chance of losing is equitable. More importantly, however, search models were used to deny the existence of involuntary unemployment and the normative basis for government intervention to prevent unemployment. Throughout the 1970s one could read in the best of economic journals such assertions as 'the unemployed worker at any time can always find some job at once' (Lucas, 1978).

Search theory denied that continued unemployment could be 'involuntary' and, in addition, some versions of implicit contract theory were used to deny the involuntary nature of an initial layoff. It was argued that workers choose firms knowing there is a probability of a future lay-off, which will be cushioned by unemployment insurance. Layoffs were seen as equivalent to occasional leisure, of little consequence since 'the typical worker who is laid off is soon rehired by his original employer' (Feldstein, 1976).

However, although the incidence of unemployment was theorized to be random and its duration short, still the waste of potential output due to unemployment might be seen as justification for stimulative macro-economic policy. To this the new labour economics replied that if one saw individuals as maximizing utility over their lifetimes, subject to the usual assumptions on foresight and capital markets, this would imply that individuals have a personally optimal lifetime total of hours of paid labour supply. Individuals may, however, alter their hours of paid labour supply in any given period, in response to perceived differences in real wages. Stimulative policies were then seen, in the short run, as inducing an increase in labour supply as individuals took advantage of a relatively high current real wage and deferred part of their lifetime consumption of leisure to a later date. In subsequent periods, however, the intertemporal substitution model of labour supply (popularized by Lucas and Rapping, 1970) argues that labour supply will decrease – hence that stimulative policies can only be of transitory benefit. Although stimulative monetary and fiscal policies could increase the supply of labour and reduce the level of unemployment (the two were seen as equivalent) by 'tricking' workers into believing that a rise in money wages was also a rise in real wages, such increases in aggregate output could not continue once the deception was discovered.

By the mid 1970s, if not before, it was no longer possible in mainstream North American literature to claim that the long-run Phillips curve was anything but vertical at the unique 'natural' rate of unemployment or, more technically, at the unique 'non-accelerating inflation rate of unemployment' (NAIRU). The NAIRU had become the most that macroeconomic policy could aim at, with the penalty attached to a more ambitious unemployment target being seen as ever accelerating inflation, while the benefits of allowing unemployment to exceed the NAIRU were seen as declining inflation and, eventually, declining inflationary expectations. However, in view of the flatness of estimated short-run expectations augmented Phillips curves (when expectations were estimated as lag functions of past wage and price inflation), it was still possible to argue that reducing inflation and inflationary expectations involved such a long and costly period of excess unemployment as to be 'on balance' undesirable. Into this breach stepped the rational expectations (RE) school. If the most rational explanation of inflation was that it was 'always and everywhere a monetary phenomenon', if people based their personal subjective expectations on such a model and if monetary policy was clearly and credibly announced in advance, RE theorists argued that inflationary expectations would adjust forthwith. Aggregate labour supply could then no longer be 'tricked' to a level above or below the NAIRU and some authors celebrated the death of the short run, as well as the long run, Phillips curve.

At this point, serious articles began to appear in reputable journals (e.g. Barro, 1977) in which workers were said to base their labour-supply decisions on the money wage and the rate of increase in the money stock permitted by the central bank authorities – variations in unemployment were 'explained' in terms of unanticipated growth in the money supply. Implicitly these articles discussed a labour market composed of homogenous individuals, without barriers to mobility, without comparisons of relative wages, without institutional constraints on wage and price setting, without collective action – indeed without institutional content of any sort. The long run collapsed into the short run and Keynesian emphasis on aggregate demand gave way to concern with microeconomic impediments to market forces such as the minimum wage. In this brave new world of deinstutionalized economics, primary emphasis was placed on monetary policy, since fiscal policy was seen as only affecting the inflation rate if mounting deficits were monetized and as otherwise having its main impact in an alteration of the share of public and private activities in the aggregate economy. However, the success of anti-inflationary policy was seen as depending crucially on central bankers' 'credibility', in that market participants would only adjust their inflationary expectations if monetary policy makers were demonstrably resolute in adhering to their announced monetary targets. Increases in unemployment following the introduction of a monetary target rule were to be ascribed by the central-bank authorities to stochastic shocks to the macroeconomy or to a lingering disbelief that the central-bank authorities really meant what they said about adhering to fixed monetary targets.*

In summary, by the end of the 1970s there had developed a substantial body of economic analysis of the labour market which denied the involuntary nature of unemployment, which argued that unemployment was not an especially inequitable or painful phenomenon in the modern economy and which held that state action to reduce unemployment could have only temporary, and not permanent, benefits. The idea of a long-run trade off between inflation and unemployment had been denied and there was a substantial body of opinion which argued that the short-run pain of disinflation could be minimized by a 'credible' policy, which implied that central-bank authorities should ignore mounting unemployment and rising bankruptcies rather than respond in a stimulative fashion, as would have been mandated by a Keynesian diagnosis.

Such an account of the 1970s should not obscure the dissenting voices that have been heard throughout this period. Indeed, in recent years, there has been something of a 'reinstitutionalization' of labour economics underway with, among other things, a re-examination of the multiple roles played by unionization and a new emphasis on the nature of long-term employment contracts, both explicit and implicit (e.g. Freeman and Medoff, 1979; Akerlof, 1980). Empirically, hard-core unemployment has been rediscovered, most notably by Clark and Summers in 1979. The persistence of low incomes among older unemployed workers and of employment status among employed workers has been emphasized by authors such as Freeman (1981) and Altonji (1982). Hall (1980) has emphasized that although individuals may hold a number of brief jobs in their first few years after leaving school, thereafter the pattern is for very infrequent job changes and near 'life-time' jobs for a large fraction of the United States labour force.

---

* In case the reader cannot credit as plausible the idea that economists should have such a view of the world or render such policy advice, he/she should consult Parkin (1982) *Modern Macro-Economics*, particularly chapters 29 and 34.

In this reinstitutionalization of labour economics, new theoretical justifications have been found for the rigid money wages and layoffs determined by seniority which are so characteristic of much blue collar employment. The theory of implicit contracts, in the context of very-long-term, 'lifetime', jobs has emphasized the complexity of interactions between rates of pay, effort, productivity and malfeasances. In macroeconomic models such as Mitchell and Kimbell (1982) the idea of overlapping contracts, with differing dates of renegotiation of wages, has been used to explain the substantial inertia which exists in the rate of wage inflation. Authors such as Solow (1980) and Lipsey (1981) have emphasized also the division of the labour market into non-competing segments, implying that unemployment may be localized and coexist for long periods of time with positive wage inflation in other segments. Macro economists who emphasize this sort of institutional impediment to the operation of market forces and continue to justify an activist government role in macroeconomic policy have often been termed 'Neo-Keynesian' but it may be a while before such viewpoints again have an influence on economic policy. Perhaps because models which explain institutional detail do not have the conceptual unity and elegance of models of human capital acquisition and search behaviour in a life time utility maximizing context, the 'new institutionalism' remains, up to the present, a minority view point within the study of labour economics. Since there are inevitable lags from the development of a 'new' perception of the nature of labour markets, to its inclusion in comprehensive macroeconomic models and to their implementation in economic policy it will likely be some time before the influence of 'new' conceptions on policy is felt.

IMPLICATIONS OF THE CURRENT 'VICTORY'

In the meantime, of course, we will face the problem of dealing with the implications of a macroeconomic policy which was largely based on a 'deinstitutionalized' view of labour markets. To some, the long-run implications of the recent recession appear minimal. It is often taken as being obvious – indeed so obvious that one need not even make it an explicit assumption – that once inflationary expectations are ground out of the system Western economies can simply return to their long-run growth paths. However, when recent experience has clearly demonstrated to an entire generation of economic decision agents that a rapid acceleration of inflation is possible, inflationary expectations can never really return to what they used to be in the 1960s. We also now know for certain that a restrictive monetary policy affects in the first instance output and not prices and that it creates extremely high rates of unemployment if pursued with sufficient rigour for a sufficiently long period of time. The high aggregate cost of this waste of resources and the inequitable distribution of the burden of unemployment are extremely strong arguments against the macroeconomic policies which produced the current recession, but since they are familiar arguments they will not be repeated here.

The emphasis here is on the impact of historically high unemployment levels on the NAIRU – that is, the impact of unemployment levels which exceed significantly, in extent and duration, the unemployment levels of 'normal' post-war cyclical downturns. Of course, even 'normal'-sized downturns affect disproportionately the unemployment rate of new entrants to the labour market and prevent the formation of human capital in the crucial early years of on-the-job training. The productive skills of unemployed older workers also suffer a sort of 'depreciation' during periods of unemployment and the low rates of capital investment during the recessionary period bequeath to future generations an older and less productive capital stock. These factors can be expected to produce a lower rate of productivity growth in future years, and exacerbate the future short-run trade-off between inflation and unemployment performance. These factors are also predictable within the context of deinstitutionalized labour economics but it is more difficult for such a perspective to deal with the institutional changes within the labour market which are likely to follow a prolonged period of high unemployment.

After all, definitions of the 'natural rate' such as that of Friedman (1968) specified

the level that would be ground out by the Walrasian system of general equilibrium equations, provided there is embedded in them the actual structural characteristics of the labour and commodity markets, including market imperfections, stochastic variability in demand and supplies, the costs of gathering information about job vacancies and labour availabilities, the costs of mobility, and so on.

However, these 'structural characteristics' and 'market imperfections' do not simply come from the sky and they are not immutably fixed. Rather they are the result of economic, political and social forces, forces which are shaped by recent economic history. Recent economic history has, in the past decade, been dominated by a series of 'incredible' events, which have necessarily shaped our current subjective estimates of the probability of future events. By 'incredible' I mean an event which was beyond the previous frame of reference of virtually all economic agents, and to which virtually no economic agents would have ascribed any positive probability. It is, for example, clear that many economic agents had the opportunity in 1977, 1978 and 1979 to choose between borrowing short or borrowing long at roughly equivalent interest rates (in North America, in the region of 10 per cent or the low teens.) Had any significant fraction of borrowers forseen the 1981 rise in interest rates, one would have observed a substantial widening of the differential interest cost of long-term borrowing in 1977–9, given the substantial advantage to be had from not having to refinance debt in 1981/82. It is quite clear that *very* few foresaw that short-term interest rates for prime borrowers would rise to over 20 per cent by late 1981 and fall by over 12 percentage points by early 1983. Many institutional features of capital markets (such as the existence of a market for long-term securities) and many organizations (such as savings and loan institutions in the United States) were previously based on the idea that these levels of interest rates, and this degree of variability of interest rates, were so unlikely as to be effectively impossible. Now that they have been proved to be possible, it is only prudent that economic agents should ensure that they are not similarly exposed in future.

Similarly, high unemployment which penetrates significantly beyond its 'traditional' populations (the young, labour force re-entrants, and permanently marginalized workers) to affect the continued existence of what were previously thought to be 'lifetime jobs' has been for many workers an 'incredible' event. The implications for their future behaviour may perhaps best be introduced by way of analogy. If a torrential downpour of rain fell for many days upon the featureless plain so beloved by economic theorists, all the inhabitants of this plain might suffer some degree of dampness but the harm to any individual would be relatively small. In the real world a prolonged torrential downpour would produce substantial amounts of flooding in low-lying areas but those individuals who live on hills or who live behind strong dykes would be relatively unaffected by the flooding. However, those without natural or man-made protections would suffer catastrophic losses. One would not expect such an event to teach individuals the lesson that, since no one would have suffered catastrophic loss had they all lived upon a featureless plain, one should destroy all dykes and level all hills. Instead, one would expect that an unexpectedly severe flood would teach the lesson that those who survive unscathed are those who live behind sufficiently tall dykes or on sufficiently high hills.

Similarly, an unemployment rate of, for example, 13 per cent, represents in many ways an object lesson in the personal benefits to an individual which can be derived from labour-market rigidities. Both the 13 per cent who are unemployed *and* the 87 per cent who are employed recognize that some workers will live through the recession almost completely unscathed. To the extent that the central-bank authorities achieve 'credibility' in their pursuit of monetary policy, we must all believe that similarly deflationary policies would be followed again in the future if inflation should again accelerate. Very few people would believe, by now, that inflation *cannot* re-accelerate should Western economies return to a higher rate of economic growth. Therefore, to the extent that we believe that central banks have attained credibility in their fight against inflation, we must also believe there is a significant probability of a return to similarly high unemployment rates in future years. In that case, the problem for an individual is to ensure that he or she will be one of those who is unscathed if there is another recession rather than one of those who are its casualities.

Even though it may be widely recognized that a more flexible labour market would entail a less-painful, short-run trade off between inflation and unemployment for the economy as a whole, this is quite irrelevant to the optimal strategy of the individual worker. The individual worker is interested in maintaining his/her own personal security under possibly deflationary conditions. As Hirschmann (1970) has pointed out, workers do not just have the market option of going elsewhere (exit) if a job situation is less than satisfactory, they also have the option of taking action (voice) to change the situation through collective bargaining, political pressure etc.

Over the years individuals have not simply used the option of 'exit' in the labour market. They have also used the option of 'voice' in order to construct a wide variety of impediments to the free play of market forces. Such labour-market institutions as the seniority system and academic or bureaucratic tenure are supplemented by the protections to local employment which can be achieved through the political mechanism, such as quotas, tariffs, local content rules and regulation. Individuals, naturally, would like to be the beneficiaries *both* of a labour-market shelter for themselves personally *and* of the efficiencies that can be produced by a freely functioning competitive economy. A tenured professor who does consulting work enjoys both employment security and the option of engaging in the market process. The advantages of possessing both security and flexibility are so obvious that attempts to gain 'tenure' are almost universal but the effort expended in the attempt depends heavily upon the strength of the expectation that its protection will be needed. In an economy with a long history of high levels of employment, one can expect job security clauses to be relatively unimportant clauses of collective agreements, one can expect fewer formal or informal guarantees of job maintenance to be made by employers and less attention to be paid by workers to the loss of seniority (and consequent loss of job security) which they incur as a result of voluntary labour-market mobility. However, although guarantees of employment security may receive less attention in a high-employment economy, they will be the focus of collective bargaining in an economy where the resurgence of high levels of unemployment is an ever-present possibility. The management of technological change is also liable to challenge as an undisputed management perogative. There is likely to be even more political pressure to enhance and maintain regulatory constraints and tariff barriers to trade.

Rigidity-increasing behaviour is, however, *not* limited to collective action. When the perceived probability of future unemployment is low, there is little cost to surrendering a guarantee of future employment. In such circumstances, declining relative wages can provide, through increased voluntary attrition, some flexibility even to those employers (such as governments and universities) which have historically provided strong employment guarantees to more senior employees. But when perceptions change, and future unemployment in another career becomes a distinct possibility, how many will voluntarily surrender tenure? Industrial workers will also begin to pay very close attention to the sacrifice of seniority which they incur as the result of a voluntary job movement. Laid-off workers are more likely to wait for recall (rather than look for jobs elsewhere) in the hope of moving up the seniority scale and avoiding future lay-offs. In short, older workers with some seniority will hold on to what they have. By doing so, each will limit the mobility alternatives open to others.

All of this occurs, of course, in the context of extremely rapid technological change, important alterations in the pattern of international trade and payments and substantial shifts in the age structure of the population. During this period, one would have hoped for a less contentious collective bargaining agenda in order to smooth the necessarily rapid pace of introduction of micro electronic and biological technology. One would have hoped, since future decades will see proportionately fewer young workers (who have traditionally been the most mobile) that at least older workers would not become more rigid and less mobile in their employment choices. One would have hoped also that developed Western economies would not attempt to shield their domestic market places from the rapidly changing realities of the international economic order. All these hopes will be frustrated to the extent that individuals are successful in their individually rational attempt to protect themselves from the credible possibility of a future recurrence of high unemployment.

In addition, there is the issue of equity and the legitimacy of the market system. Laidler and Rowe are among those who have argued for the importance of price stability for the 'promotion and preservation of the trust upon which a free economic order depends' (1980: 104). They and others have argued that the efficiences of a market organization of economic life cannot in the long run be had if the inequities of inflation undermine confidence in the market mechanism. But if we reject controls as a method of controlling inflation and prefer to grind inflation out of the economic system with excess capacity and unemployment, one can legitimately wonder if belief in the efficacy of the market mechanism is more quickly eroded by unemployment than by inflation.

The conundrum is that, as the current recession is teaching us, monetary restraint produces lower rates of core inflation only when the collapse of aggregate demand threatens the 'life-time' jobs of the established workers who dominate the wage-bargaining process. However, the actual loss of such jobs can be, for such older workers, a financial disaster — in income loss while unemployed, in possible loss of pension entitlements or home equity and in lowered wages when re-employed (see Freeman, 1981; 151). Psychologists have also documented the cycle of shock, constructive activity, inactivity/depression and eventual adaptation to unemployed status through which the unemployed normally pass (see Hayes and Nutman 1981). Those who emphasize only the economic aspects of unemployment may choose to see it as an inability to make a market trade at one's desired price, involving the same sort of loss of utility as the inability to sell one's car at one's initial asking price, but unemployment is clearly much more than that. Unemployment affects basic ideas of self-conception and self-esteem and it alters social relationships within the family and with the larger society. Unless it is of short duration, such as a layoff with quick recall or a quickly successful search, or unless it is experienced as part of one's initial 'job-shopping' in the labour market, unemployment is a profoundly important event to an individual — in the current context, to many individuals. Individuals have to find some way of explaining such an event to themselves. Should unemployment remain at relatively high levels, it will become much easier for the unemployed to see themselves as faultless victims of a faulty system rather than underserving deviants in an essentially sound system.

As discussed earlier, however, high rates of unemployment affect the institutional behaviour of both the employed and the unemployed. The vast majority, now as in the Great Depression, remain employed and their attitudes toward the market mechanism will be essential for its survival. A heightened sense of insecurity among the employed, especially if combined with stagnant real incomes, is likely to create intense political strains but whether these strains tend to produce radicalism of the 'right' or of the 'left' is an issue which is far from clear and whose analysis lies far beyond the scope of this essay. I would, however, argue that one can only expect the combination of liberal democracy and a mixed enterprise market economy to remain unscathed by prolonged high unemployment to the extent that the bulk of the population can reasonably expect to remain unscathed by prolonged high unemployment — i.e. to the extent that they can construct for themselves their own personal labour-market shelters. If 'voice' cannot produce an acceptable combination of security and income within one institutional structure, it is likely to be used to produce another.

CONCLUSION

This essay has argued that part of the reason why we have such high unemployment rates in the early 1980s is the economic analysis of unemployment which took place in the 1960s and 1970s. This analysis reinterpreted 'typical' unemployment in terms of voluntary maximizing behaviour in a competitive market context and, although references were sometimes made to 'minority groups and the hard-to-employ', their involuntary unemployment was seen as a distinctly subsidiary and separate issue. Unemployment became viewed as primarily a short-term phenomenon — 'a normal state in the labour market through which most workers pass' (Addison and Siebert, 1980). As a consequence, the prevention of unemployment received much less emphasis as a policy goal — a weighting of policy objectives which would have seemed incredible to a labour economist of the early 1960s.

The 'new' view of unemployment carried the day only partly because of its theoretical elegance and compatibility with standard micro-economic tools. It was also successful partly because the sort of frictional unemployment which it describes so well, and whose existence many generations of economists had admitted, *was* more or less a good description of unemployment in large urban labour markets during periods of very high capacity utilization (as in the US in the late 1960s). Unemployment in depressed regions or during significant contractions of money output presents, however, quite different issues. Unless we recognize these differences in the nature of unemployment we will not recognize that the most appropriate model of unemployment to use will depend on the economic context in which that unemployment occurs. Until we recognize that the mechanism by which wages are set and adjusted differ (e.g. between union and non-union sectors and between 'primary. and 'secondary' workers) we will misestimate the response of wage inflation and unemployment to money-demand contraction.

If these misestimates were only 'academic' issues, one could argue that none of this would matter much, but I would argue that we are now seeing in economic policy some of the costs of the loss of perspective among economists that comes with a refusal to perceive qualitative differences in the labour market and a reluctance to recognize that models of the labour market which are appropriate in one context are not appropriate in another. The costs of these misperceptions are very serious. As Pyrrhus discovered, many years ago, a misperception of the costs of a battle can turn a successful campaign into a disastrous war, and the longer one persists in the misperception the greater is the disaster.

POSTSCRIPT

During 1983 Britain, the United States, Canada and Germany began to recover from the 1981/82 world recession. Unemployment fell in North America but, at 9 per cent in the United States and 11 per cent in Canada, remained very high by historical standards. In Europe, unemployment rates averaged over 10 per cent and either remained constant or rose slightly. In all countries, medium-term forecasts were extremely pessimistic about the possibility of lowering unemployment appreciably. Despite a continued decline in current inflation, fears of future inflation continued, based in part on the persistence of high United States budget deficits, in part on the responsiveness of commodity prices to increased aggregate demand and in part on fears of renewed union militancy on wages.

What is one to make of a mild recovery with high unemployment and continued worries of inflation? In particular, what lessons has labour learned from the recession? In the deinstitutionalized world of many macro-economic models it is presumed that labour learns only to adjust inflationary expectations and, therefore, will accept lower nominal wage increases. In the real world, however, labour learns about quantity as well as price adjustments, about political as well as economic processes.

Politically, the major lesson of the recession is that governments can be re-elected despite levels of unemployment which even a few years ago would have been considered intolerable. As a result, the credibility of anti-inflationary policies has increased, since a major deterrent to such policies has been fear of electoral defeat. The major economic lesson has been that price deflation *is* possible, although only at the cost of substantial unemployment. These lessons, plus continued apprehensions about a resurgence of inflationary pressures, mean that one must take very seriously the possibility that unemployment will return to levels of 13—15 per cent as the next phase of a 'stop—go' cycle.

During the 'go' phase of the cycle (which the United States, at least, was entering by late 1983) unions have a degree of bargaining power and can 'spend', in a sense, that power on obtaining either higher wages or better job-security clauses. Individuals similarly have more options in good times and can trade off income and security in their job choices. The possibility of a future anti-inflation recession of comparable magitude to the last one increases the incentives for labour to opt for job security, to build stronger, more rigid protections against the chance of future unemployment.

The problem for modern economies is that labour market rigidities are a large part of the reason why contractionary demand policies are so expensive, in lost output, as a way of decreasing inflation. One cannot, however, piously hope for such rigidities to decrease since they represent, in many cases, significant protections against unemployment for the people concerned. Periods of high unemployment send the clear signal that such protections against unemployment are valuable. Each use of contractionary demand policies to decrease inflation therefore tends to increase the labour market rigidities which make such policies so expensive. Should inflationary pressures re-emerge, the next recession will have to be even more severe than the last, if it is to achieve a similar 'victory' over inflation.

REFERENCES

Addison, J. T. and Siebert, W. S. (1979) *The Market for Labor: An Analytical Approach*, Santa Monica, Goodyear Publishing Co.

Akerlof, G. A. (1980), A theory of social custom, of which unemployment may be one consequence, *Quarterly Journal of Economics*, XCIV, 4, 749–76.

Altonji, J. G. (1982), The intertemporal substitution model of labour market fluctuations: An empirical analysis, *The Review of Economic Studies*, XLIX, 159, Special Issue, 783–824.

Baily, M. N. (ed.) (1982) *Workers, Jobs and Inflation*, The Brookings Institution: Washington DC.

Barro, R. J. Unanticipated money growth and unemployment in the United States, *The American Economic Review*, 67, 2 101–15.

Bouey, G. K. (1982) Monetary policy – finding a place to stand, (Per Jacobsson Lecture), *Bank of Canada Review*, September, 3–18.

Clark, K. B. and Summers, L. H. (1979) Labor market dynamics and unemployment: A reconsideration, *Brookings Papers on Economic Activity*, 1, 13–60, The Brookings Institution, Washington, DC.

Feldstein, M. S. (1976) Temporary layoffs in the theory of unemployment, *Journal of Political Economy,* **84**, 5, 937–58.

Feldstein, M. S. (1979) The welfare cost of permanent inflation and optimal short run economic policy, *Journal of Political Economy*, **87**, 4, 749–68.

Freeman, R. B. (1981) *Troubled Workers in the Labor Market*, Working Paper 816, Cambridge: National Bureau of Economic Research.

Freeman, R. B. and Medoff, J. L. (1979) The Two Faces of Unionism, *The Public Interest*, 57.

Friedman, M. (1968) The role of monetary policy, *American Economic Review*, LVII, 1, 1–17.

Gordon, R. J. (1982) Inflation flexible exchange rates and the natural rate of unemployment. In M. N. Baily (ed.) *Workers, Jobs and Inflation*, The Brookings Institution: Washington, DC, 89–152.

Hall, R. E. (1980) *The Importance of Lifetime Jobs in the U.S. Economy*, New York: NBER, Working Paper Series No. 560.

Hayes, J. and Nutman, P. (1981) *Understanding the Unemployed: The Psychological Effects of Unemployment*, London: Tavistock Publications.

Hirschmann, A. O. (1970) *Exit Voice and Loyalty*, Cambridge: Harvard University Press.

Kerr, C. (1950) Labor Markets: Their character and consequence, *American Economic Review*, May.

Laidler, D. and Rowe, N. (1980) On Simmel, *Journal of Economic Literature*, XVIII, 97–105.

Lipsey, R. G. (1981) The understanding and control of inflation: Is there a crisis in macroeconomics, *Canadian Journal of Economics*, **14**, 4, 545–76.

Lucas, R. E. Jr. (1978) Unemployment policy, *American Economic Review*, **68**, 2, 353–7.

Lucas, R. and Rapping L. (1970) Real wages, employment and inflation. In Phelps (ed.) *Microeconomic Foundations of Employment and Inflation Theory*, W. W. Norton: New York, 257–308.

Mitchell, P. J. B. and Kimball, L. J. (1982) Labor market contracts and inflation. In M. N. Baily (ed.) *Workers, Jobs and Inflation*, The Brookings Institution, Washington, DC, 199–238.

Nordhaus, W. D. (1973) The effects of inflation on the distribution of economic welfare, *Journal of Money Credit and Banking*, V, 1, Part II, 465–504.

Okun, A. M. (1978) Efficient disinflationary policies, *American Economic Review*, **68**, 2, 348–52.

Okun, A. M. (1981) *Prices and Quantities: A Macro-Economic Analysis*, Oxford: Basil Blackwell.

Parkin, M. J. (1982) *Modern Macro Economics*, Prentice-Hall: Scarborough.

Phelps, E. S. (ed.) (1970) *Microeconomic Foundations of Employment and Inflation Theory*, W. W. Norton: New York.

Reynolds, L. (1951) *The Structure of Labor Markets, Wages and labour Mobility: Theory and Practice*, Westport, Connecticut: Greenwood Press.

Solow, R. M. (1980) On theories of unemployment, *The American Economic Review*, **70**, 1, 1–11.

Tobin, J. (1972) Inflation and unemployment, *The American Economic Review*, LXII, 1, 1–18.

Woods, H. D. and Ostry, S. (1962) *Labour Policy and Labour Economics in Canada*, Toronto: Macmillan.

7

International Aspects of Stagflation

A. M. SINCLAIR

INTRODUCTION

Within three years of Nixon's August 15, 1971 announcement that the United States dollar–gold link was broken, the Bretton Woods system of fixed but adjustable exchange rates was replaced by a system of flexible but managed exchange rates. This has been accompanied by profound changes in the economic performance of industrial and third-world economies. Most of these changes have been for the worst: falling rates of increase in productivity, rising rates of inflation, high levels of unemployment, sharply rising energy prices and falling terms of trade for non-oil-producing developing countries.

This paper looks beyond the problem of the impact of unemployment on inflation to consider the policy problems that will arise when unemployment has increased sufficiently to bring down the rate of inflation. In particular, it focuses upon the balance-of-payments constraint upon economic recovery in a world where large OPEC surpluses are likely to reappear unless measures are taken to prevent the price of oil from rising.

Stagflation in Europe and in North America has been partially sustained by balance-of-payments factors, since countries that seek to reflate can find themselves in balance-of-payments difficulties. Canada, with ready access to the United States capital market, has been less affected by balance-of-payments constraints on growth than European countries in general, but Canada has nevertheless experienced difficult economic circumstances in the later 1970s and 1980s.

The purpose of this essay is two-fold. First, the case for an aggressive use of the foreign exchange rate as part of an anti-

---

I should like to acknowledge helpful comments from J. Cornwall, M. Cross, T. Eisenhauer, L. Osberg and B. Lesser. Errors remain my responsibility

recession package is argued. The exchange rate is a particularly important instrument of policy if a country wishes to stimulate aggregate demand unilaterally. However, an underlying assumption of the analysis is that some form of an incomes policy, probably of the tax-based nature, will also be necessary in order to prevent demand stimulation from resulting in continued or renewed inflation. Secondly, the overall balance of payments constraint that would arise at full employment in the world as a whole, resulting from the existence of OPEC surpluses, requires that some solution to the oil-shock problem be implemented if high rates of economic growth are to be attained. Some of these options are considered in the latter part of the paper.

The use of the exchange rate as a device to stimulate output and growth has been rejected by some economists because it is argued that the exchange rate has no influence on real variables. This argument is considered in the second section. The third section deals with the question as to whether the exchange rate is simply a non-tariff barrier. Some empirical estimates for the United States, Sweden, Canada and Britain on the impact of a change in the exchange rate is provided in the fourth section. The paper concludes with a discussion of the OPEC balance-of-payments constraint and of ways by which its impact might be minimized in future years.

THE EXCHANGE RATE AND REAL VARIABLES

Classical analysis of the price-specie flow balance-of-payments mechanism under fixed exchange rates, associated with the name of David Hume, suggested that a country with a balance-of-payments surplus would experience an increase in its price level, owing to an inflow of gold. This increase in the price level would then tend to make exports less competitive and imports more competitive, putting downward pressure on the balance-of-payments surplus. The gold exchange system was thus self-equilibrating.

Modern theorists, led by Mundell, have pointed to a logical flaw in the Hume analysis, at least as summarized in the conventional manner (Mundell, 1968: chap 8). In a world of fixed exchange rates and perfect competition, the prices of goods are equalized throughout the world by commodity arbitrage, ignoring transport costs. The price level *per se* cannot rise in one country, or, more specifically, the price of product A in the surplus country cannot rise above the price of the same product A in the deficit country, where product A can be taken as either an export or an import product from the perspective of the surplus country. One solution to this problem is to argue that expenditure changes following from the balance of payments surplus of country X will cause the prices of the goods that X exports to rise (in both countries) and the prices of its imports to fall. Relative prices thus return as the instrument of balance of payments adjustment.

In the real world of flexible exchange rates and imperfect competition, the commodity arbitrage assumption is still often used to examine the impact of a devaluation or depreciation in an exchange rate upon the prices of tradeable goods. In general, a 10 per cent fall in the price of a currency will tend to *raise* the price of exports in terms of domestic currency by 10 per cent or less (with zero as a limit), depending upon its share of the market of the good in question, and the 10 per cent devaluation will tend to *lower* the price of exports in terms of foreign currency by from 0 to 10 per cent. Commodity arbitrage in this case would ensure that the absolute sum of the increase in terms of domestic currency plus the decrease in terms of foreign currency equals exactly 10 per cent, the extent of the exchange-rate change. Similarly, the devaluation will tend to *raise* the price of imports in terms of domestic currency and *lower* the price of imports in terms of foreign currency, again by a total of 10 per cent. For a small country with no impact on the price of any tradeable product, a 10 per cent devaluation, given commodity arbitrage, would result in a 10 per cent increase in the price in terms of domestic currency of both exports and imports, and no change in the price in terms of foreign currency of either exports or imports. The relative price on world markets of this country's exports and imports is unchanged by the devaluation. Only the domestic nominal prices of exports and imports will have changed for this small country. It is clear that the usual journalistic description of a devaluation as tending to reduce the price of exports and to raise the price of imports fails to distinguish the currency in which prices are quoted and is, therefore, quite misleading.

The law of one price, which is implied by commodity arbitrage, has been tested and shown not to hold for all traded goods (Isard, 1977; Kravis and Lipsey, 1977). In the context of devaluation, a relevant question is whether or not changes in relative prices reflect the degree of devaluation as described above, even if absolute prices differ for a variety of reasons. Some evidence suggests that even limited commodity arbitrage, given exchange-rate changes, is not universal. For example, the British press noted that a 20 per cent devaluation of the pound in terms of the yen in the late 1970s led to no change in the sterling price of certain Japanese cars in Britain, and, by implication, no change in the yen price of cars in Japan. Limited evidence for Canada shows that, for certain products, such as newsprint and whiskey, substantial changes in the exchange rate between Canada and the United States during the later 1970s had no effect on prices quoted in domestic currency in either country for a considerable period.

However, whether the law of one price holds because markets are competitive, or whether market reactions are muted and slow, a devaluation, the effect of which on relative prices, if any, is concentrated on tradeable goods, will result in expenditure-switching behaviour. This expenditure switching will tend to increase the output of exports and reduce the volume of imports. As is well known, the effects on total values, or the balance-of-trade effects, depend upon demand and supply elasticities, but the direct output or employment effects are more certain. Even in those cases where relative prices do not shift at all as a result of devaluation it is probable that economic activity is affected, at least in one country: e.g. the incentive for Japan to export cars to Britain at a fixed sterling price in the face of a 20 per cent devaluation of sterling, given constant yen prices, is reduced to some degree.

Commodity arbitrage across borders is thus not a reason for believing that devaluations simply wash themselves out in price increases. What is needed for this result to follow is what may be termed internal commodity arbitrage – i.e. an increase in the price of exports and of imports in terms of domestic currency is accompanied by (an immediate) increase in the price of all non-tradeables, thus eliminating balance-of-trade and expenditure-switching effects, and thus leaving real output and employment unchanged. While many authors have noted that devaluation can be a futile exercise in terms of impacting on real output and employment, this is not an inevitable result. In general, a devaluation undertaken at full employment without due consideration to reducing domestic absorption to release resources in order to increase exports will simply cause an equal and completely offsetting price inflation. But a devaluation undertaken at less than full employment need not have this result unless prices of non-tradeables, including money wages, are quickly responsive to rises in the price of tradeables. In some situations of rapid inflation this is, of course, what does happen — in Israel, menus in quite modest restaurants have prices indicated in United States dollars, payment in shekels to be made at that day's exchange rate. But in general, even in the double-digit inflation of OECD countries in recent years, devaluations do change relative prices of tradeables as against non-tradeables, and they do, or can, have a real impact on output and employment. Some evidence of this is provided below.

From a policy perspective, in contemporary situations it would probably be useful for 'labour' and 'management' to agree that the direct impact of devaluation on the cost of living be excluded from the bargaining process, since indexing of such real changes in the terms of trade can clearly be explosive (Gordon, 1978: 326). Such agreement would have to form part of a 'comprehensive' and 'fair' incomes policy, however. A possible reason for labour to agree to make such a bargain would be that labour would gain in real terms if and when the exchange rate were to appreciate. But even without this agreement a devaluation under conditions of substantial unemployment can increase real output and employment. In the aggregate labour might be said to gain in this case, but some individuals will lose (e.g. those who do not experience unemployment but who pay more for imported goods) and others will gain (e.g. those who obtain jobs that they would not otherwise obtain).

DEPRECIATION AND TARIFFS AS FORMS OF PROTECTION

In a long-run general equilibrium context a tax on imports will have equivalent effects to a tax on exports, but in a short-run, unemployment context a tax on imports is equivalent in its effects to a subsidy on exports (Chacholiades, 1978: chap. 17). A devaluation in turn is a device for simultaneously taxing imports and subsidizing exports. Despite their formal similarity, taxes and subsidies on the one hand and devaluations on the other have quite different political and economic ramifications in practice. In political terms, tariffs and subsidies are restricted by GATT, whereas exchange rates since 1973 and indeed since 1945 are largely outside the scope of formal political 'third party' intermediation. As will be discussed subsequently, this inability to discuss exchange rates within a multinational environment is a serious flaw in our present-day economic armoury. However, on

International Aspects of Stagflation

economic grounds it is instructive to note that tariffs and subsidies as control mechanisms do differ in important ways from devaluations, and that these ways may explain some of the differential political attention paid to these instruments. (The IMF was established to monitor and control exchange-rate movements and to allow changes in response to undefined 'fundamental disequilibria'. While it has performed a useful subsidiary lending role, the IMF has never been able to prevent exchange-rate movements in practice, and certainly cannot do so today. Canada is just one of many countries whose exchange-rate policies violated IMF rules in the 1950s, for example.)

Despite their possible theoretical equivalence, there are five reasons why devaluations for reflationary objectives can be considered superior to a combination of tariffs and subsidies on grounds of economic efficiency.

1. A tariff-cum-subsidy scheme has high administrative costs, both in terms of the cost of dispensing information and in terms of the cost of administering the programmes. The transaction costs associated with a devaluation are less, since the price system is used to transmit information and to enforce the impact on expenditures.
2. A tariff-cum-subsidy scheme has significant cash-flow implications for government budgets, whereas the direct impact on government budgets of a devaluation is less. Government expenditure in domestic currency will increase only for imports and for servicing foreign debt denominated in foreign currency.
3. Tariffs and subsidies are not in practice uniformly applied across all commodities, and services are almost universally excluded. 'Tariff escalation' gives rise to high rates of effective protection on finished products, for example. A devaluation impinges equally on all commodities, and on services as well as commodities, and therefore introduces fewer distortions or side effects into an economy.
4. Tariffs and subsidies invite corruption, whereas a devaluation unaccompanied by increased exchange control minimizes corruption possibilities. The problem of corruption can be acute, as the case of many developing countries can attest. Ghana presents an extreme example of the problem.
5. Generally, a devaluation can have a quicker impact than tarriffs-cum-subsidies, since the administrative time lag is shorter. So-called 'J effects' on the balance of trade and stickiness of

actual prices in response to policy induced changes are equally probable under either system.

It can be argued that the theoretical equivalence of a tariff-cum-subsidy scheme with a devaluation misses the real point, which is that an import tariff alone (or combined with other restrictions on imports such as quotas and advance deposits) is the practical alternative to a devaluation. However, only point 2 above would be significantly altered by this consideration: a tariff alone would increase government revenue directly, whereas a devaluation would raise government expenditure directly.

Finally, elaborate arguments have been developed to contend that the price mechanism quickly washes away the real effects of a devaluation, as discussed earlier. Few if any have ever argued that the effects of tariffs, or of tariffs-cum-subsidies, are similarly washed away. This might be taken as an economic argument in favour of tariffs-cum-subsidies, except that the position that devaluations are quickly washed away in all circumstances is extreme and unwarranted.

The general conclusion is that devaluation is a preferable policy to a tariff-cum-subsidy scheme to influence the trade balance on economic grounds, and therefore a better instrument with which to reflate. On political grounds, there seems no question but that devaluation raises fewer problems than a tariff-cum-subsidy scheme, or simply a tariff policy. However, this point can be overstated: in late 1982 it was reported that eight steel producers in the United States had asked for a 25 per cent tariff duty on Japanese steel imports, owing among other things to the undervaluation of the Japanese yen.

THE REAL IMPACT OF EXCHANGE RATE ALTERATIONS

Theoretical and empirical study of the impact of a change in the exchange rate has been extensive, in part because the exchange rate is usually one of the most important prices in an economy with ramifications for economic decision-making relating to production, investment and financial flows. In addition, the exchange rate is in turn influenced by production decisions, by real investment, and by financial flows, including government borrowing. In order to reduce the complexity of the real world, a number of authors recently have placed a great emphasis on the link between government deficits and the trade balance in a way which tends to reduce the potential for using the exchange rate to influence aggregate demand. A recent review article by McKinnon (1981) is an important statement of this position, and it is used as an illustration of this influential school of thought.

McKinnon's theoretical and empirical analysis of the United States economy in the 1970s leads him to conclude that the effect of a real devaluation of the dollar on the Unites States economy is ambiguous (and, by implication, the effect of a real appreciation of the dollar in the United States economy would be ambiguous). McKinnon's analysis is essentially a variant of the absorption approach, incorporating price changes and real balance effects. The key conclusion of the absorption, approach to a devaluation is that the balance of trade $(X - M)$ can improve if, and only if, there is an increase in net private-sector saving $(S - I)$ or in public-sector saving $(T - G)$. If, for example, a devaluation is undertaken at full employment and a complementary constraining policy involving tighter monetary and fiscal policy does not accompany the devaluation, then no domestically consumed output will be released for exports (and no imports will be reduced, since they are included in domestically consumed output or absorption), and hence the balance of trade will not be improved. This result is well known to economists, but because the implication is often not accepted by policymakers, many devaluations have not succeeded in improving the trade balance.

The specific details of McKinnon's analysis are nevertheless of interest since they represent an important school of thought. McKinnon assumes that the economy is at full employment, or at least that unemployment (U) equals its natural rate $(U)_n$. His basic hypothesis is that a real devaluation does tend to increase *public*-sector net saving, but *private*-sector net saving tends to fall, so the net effect is ambiguous. Since $U = U_n$, a real devaluation, unanticipated, increases both the price level and real output. Both of these will increase tax revenues relative to government expenditure, so $(T - G)$ is increased. Private-sector saving, which might be expected to increase, owing to the real balance effect of an increased price level, is unchanged (relative to income) since the real balance effect is offset by consumption expenditures induced by expectations of inflation. Private-sector investment increases as a result of the devaluation, mainly because multinational firms see a temporary and artificial fall in United States costs. Presumably the argument is that a German mark, say, can, *ceteris paribus*, purchase more real physical assets in the United States because prices and costs there have not risen proportionately to the devaluation, at least in the short run.

Before looking at the empirical evidence, it is worth noting that within the full-employment tradition, McKinnon's conclusion regarding investment is suspect since investment in new real physical assets is only warranted if real output is permanently increased, and this possibility is denied when $U = U_n$. However, if full employment is not assumed, McKinnon's conclusion regarding investment is strengthened, since investment in new real physical assets in the United States will be attractive not only to those operating within a world-wide perspective, but to domestic United States firms which see prospects of increased sales.

McKinnon states that the evidence for the 1970s is consistent with a stable S/Y ratio for the United States. These numbers are implicit in his Table 2, but they are not explicitly calculated. The saving ratios are included here in Table 7.1, which reproduces his figure for I, $(T - G)$ and $(X - M)$ for 1971-9 for the United States, but which also extends the figures to 1981, and which adds similar figures for Britain, Sweden and Canada. All figures are taken as proportions of Gross National Product. Table 7.2 shows changes in effective exchange rates over the period from 1971–82 for the four countries, and Table 7.3 shows changes in consumer prices. The effective exchange rate is a weighted average of the exchange rate between a currency and 17 other major currencies, where the weights reflect the size of trade flows as well as the impact of exchange-rate changes on these trade flows. (See IMF, *International Financial Statistics, 1981 Yearbook*, pp. 4–5.)

If the S ratio is constant, and if the I ratio increases with a fall in the exchange rate, then the hypothesis advanced by McKinnon is that the change in $(S - I)$ following a devaluation will be negative. As noted previously, McKinnon also hypothesizes that the change in $(T - G)$ will be positive. These results are observed in the United States data for the only case considered in detail by McKinnon, 1977/78, during which period the effective exchange rate fell by 8.6 per cent. Since $(T - G)$ increased by 0.006 (i.e. from -0.027 to -0.021) and $(S - I)$ fell by the same amount, the trade balance remained unchanged despite the devaluation (McKinnon, 1981: 545). McKinnon (1981: 546) argues that this evidence and other results support the view that 'the most direct instrument of official policy for influencing the trade balance is the state of the public finances: the balance between revenues and expenditures. The

Table 7.1 *Private investment, public-sector saving, trade balance and saving as proportions of GNP, 1971–81*

	1971	1972	1973	1974	1975	1976	1977	1978	1979	1980	1981
Canada											
I	0.224	0.224	0.238	0.256	0.241	0.243	0.232	0.229	0.247	0.232	0.249
$T - G$	−0.018	−0.017	−0.014	−0.011	−0.031	−0.028	−0.034	−0.050	−0.039	−0.038	−0.025
$X - M$	0.019	0.008	0.013	0.002	−0.015	−0.005	−0.001	−0.003	−0.007	0.017	0.011
S	0.261	0.249	0.265	0.269	0.257	0.266	0.265	0.282	0.293	0.287	0.285
Sweden											
I	0.231	0.221	0.214	0.238	0.241	0.237	0.202	0.176	0.202	0.216	0.187
$T - G$	−0.013	−0.014	−0.025	−0.030	−0.015	−0.011	−0.036	−0.066	−0.083	−0.091	n.a.
$X - M$	0.012	0.015	0.028	−0.008	−0.002	−0.017	0.017	0.011	−0.010	−0.018	−0.003
S	0.256	0.250	0.267	0.260	0.254	0.231	0.221	0.253	0.275	0.289	n.a.
Britain											
I	0.185	0.182	0.211	0.214	0.179	0.194	0.192	0.182	0.190	0.160	n.a.
$T - G$	−0.011	−0.025	−0.032	−0.041	−0.079	−0.054	−0.031	−0.051	−0.054	−0.050	n.a.
$X - M$	0.014	−0.001	−0.624	−0.051	−0.017	−0.012	−0.007	−0.013	−0.003	−0.024	n.a.
S	0.210	0.206	0.219	0.204	0.241	0.236	0.230	0.250	0.247	0.234	n.a.
United States											
I	0.150	0.161	0.168	0.152	0.124	0.143	0.160	0.165	0.163	0.153	0.161
$T - G$	−0.023	−0.015	−0.007	−0.009	−0.049	−0.033	−0.027	−0.021	−0.012	−0.026	−0.025
$X - M$	−0.005	−0.009	−0.001	−0.006	0.006	−0.003	−0.015	−0.015	−0.013	−0.008	−0.008
S	0.168	0.167	0.174	0.155	0.179	0.173	0.172	0.171	0.162	0.171	0.178

Sources: United States figures for 1971-9 are from McKinnon (1981) Table 2, p. 543. (The figure for *S* is calculated from the others, since $S = I - (T - G) + (X - M)$.) The 1980 and 1981 United States figures, and all figures for Canada, Sweden and Britain, are from International Monetary Fund, *International Financial Statistics*, 1982 Yearbook, Country Tables. All figures are expressed as a proportion of GNP on line 99a. Figures for *I* appear in lines 93e (93ee for the United States) and 93i. Figures for $(T - G)$ are on line 80, and for $(X - M)$ on line 90c minus line 98c. *S* is calculated as a residual, as noted earlier.

Table 7.2 Percentage change in effective exchange rates, 1971–82

	Canada	Sweden	UK	US
1971/72	−1.0	1.4	−3.9	−7.1
1972/73	−4.9	0.6	−10.0	−8.3
1973/74	3.4	−0.3	−2.8	2.3
1974/75	−4.6	4.7	−7.7	−1.1
1975/76	6.1	0.3	−14.4	5.2
1976/77	−7.6	−3.5	−5.1	−0.5
1977/78	−10.4	−8.0	0.4	−8.6
1978/79	−4.0	2.2	7.0	−2.1
1979/80	0.2	1.2	10.2	0.2
1980/81	2.8	−5.3	−1.2	12.6
1981/82	4.5	−18.6	−2.8	17.2

Source: Calculated from IMF, *International Financial Statistics*, 1982 Yearbook, Country Tables, line am x. For 1982, the October figure is used, from *International Financial Statistics*, December 1982.

consequences of adjusting the exchange rates are unpredictable.'

The traditional analysis of a devaluation, such as that experienced by the United States in 1977/78, is that exports will increase and that imports may increase or decrease, since substitution and income effects work in opposite directions. If import demand elasticities are high enough, and if the marginal propensity to

Table 7.3 Percentage change in consumer prices, 1971–82

	Canada	Sweden	UK	US
1971/72	4.8	6.0	12.8	3.3
1972/73	7.5	6.7	13.5	6.3
1973/74	10.9	9.9	17.7	10.9
1974/75	10.7	9.8	26.6	9.2
1975/76	7.5	10.3	15.5	5.8
1976/77	8.0	11.4	10.3	6.5
1977/78	9.0	9.9	14.6	7.5
1978/79	9.2	7.3	15.3	11.3
1979/80	10.1	13.7	18.7	13.5
1980/81	12.4	12.1	13.4	10.4
1981/82	12.9	9.6	5.7	7.6

Source: Calculated from sources noted in Table 2. Line 64 is used. The 1982 figure is for September.

import is not too high, the trade balance will tend to improve. In the short run it is recognized that import elasticities may be very low, resulting in the well-known J-curve effect. These traditional results are denied by the school of thought represented by McKinnon. Part of the difference is only apparent, however. There is general recognition that under conditions of full employment a devaluation, unaccompanied by any appropriate monetary or fiscal policy, is bound to fail. Part of the difference relates to the choice of countries and circumstances, since institutional differences can be important in assessing the impact of a devaluation. For example, the indexing of the personal income tax in Canada would tend to modify the conclusion that a devaluation will increase T. Since full employment is obviously not a reasonable general assumption, and since institutional differences among countries are important, it is necessary to look carefully at a number of examples before drawing strong conclusions concerning the real impact of exchange-rate adjustments.

In order to obtain some feel for the robustness of McKinnon's hypotheses, 17 significant annual movements in effective exchange rates involving Canada, Sweden, Britain and the United States are analysed in Table 7.4, including the 1977/78 movement in the United States dollar. The results suggest great caution in accepting McKinnon's results. Table 1 suggests that the S ratio is not particularly stable for countries outside the United States. The evidence in Table 7.4 shows that falling exchange rates were accompanied by reduced $(S - I)$ ratios (or rising exchange rates by increased $(S - I)$ ratios) in only 7 of the 17 exchange-rate revisions examined. Similarly, McKinnon's hypothesis that a falling exchange rate will be accompanied by an increased $(T - G)$ ratio (or a rising exchange rate with a reduced $(T - G)$ ratio) is found to be valid for only 7 of the 17 cases examined.

Overall, the trade balance ratio $(X - M)$ moved in the 'correct' direction on 10 of 17 occasions (i.e. a depreciation was accompanied by an increase and an appreciation by a decrease). The $(X - M)$ ratio moved the incorrect way on five occasions, and on two occasions it did not move.

The most interesting result in the context of a less than fully employed economy concerns the movement in the ratio of exports alone to GNP. The X ratio moved in the 'correct' direction following 16 of the 17 devaluations – that is to say, a depreciation was accompanied by an increase in the X ratio and an appreciation by a decrease (see Table 7.4). The only exception to this is the

Table 7.4 Selected changes in effective exchange rates for four countries, 1971–81, and associated changes in $(S − I)$, $(T − G)$, $(X − M)$, X and M

Country	Years	Movement in effective exchange rate	Change in components of private- and public-sector net saving and in trade balance				
			$(S − I)$	$(T − G)$	$(X − M)$	X	M
Canada	1972/73	−4.9	+0.002	+0.003	−0.005	+0.015	+0.010
	1975/76	+6.1	+0.007	+0.003	−0.010	−0.003	−0.013
	1976/77	−7.6	+0.010	−0.006	−0.004	+0.012	+0.008
	1977/78	−10.4	+0.020	−0.016	+0.004	+0.021	0.017
Sweden	1974/75	+4.7	−0.009	+0.015	+0.006	−0.040	−0.046
	1977/78	−8.0	+0.058	−0.030	+0.028	+0.009	−0.018
Britain	1972/73	−10.0	−0.016	−0.007	−0.023	+0.017	+0.041
	1974/75	−7.7	−0.072	−0.038	+0.034	−0.017	−0.049
	1975/76	−14.4	−0.020	+0.025	+0.005	+0.024	+0.018
	1976/77	−5.1	−0.004	+0.023	+0.019	+0.022	+0.003
	1978/79	+7.0	−0.007	−0.003	−0.010	−0.003	+0.008
	1979/80	+10.2	+0.017	+0.004	+0.021	−0.004	−0.026
United States	1971/72	−7.1	−0.012	+0.008	−0.004	+0.001	+0.004
	1972/73	−8.3	0.000	+0.008	+0.008	+0.013	+0.006
	1975/76	+5.2	−0.025	−0.016	−0.009	−0.001	+0.009
	1977/78	−8.6	−0.006	−0.006	0.000	+0.003	+0.002
	1980/81	+12.6	−0.001	+0.001	0.000	−0.004	−0.004

Sources: Movement in effective exchange rates as in Table 7.2. Changes in $(S − I)$, $(T − G)$ and $(X − M)$ are calculated from Table 7.1. Changes in X and M are calculated from sources given in Table 1. The figures for the United States were calculated using the revised estimates in the 1982 *IMF Yearbook*. These estimates differ slightly from those used by McKinnon in calculating $(X − M)$ for the United States, using the 1980 *IMF Yearbook*.

Note: All figures, X and M included, are given as a proportion of GNP. Algebraically, the change in $(S − I)$ plus the change in $(T − G)$ equals the change in $(X − M)$. Discrepancies here are the result of rounding errors, or, in the case of the United States from 1971 to 1979, because different sources are used for $(X − M)$ and for X and M, as noted above.

British depreciation of 1974/75, which was accompanied by a fall in the X ratio of 0.017. Also noteworthy is that the change in the X ratio was accompanied by a change in the M ratio in the same direction in 14 of the 17 cases considered. For example, in the 1972/73 depreciation in Canada the X ratio rose by 0.015 and the M ratio also increased, by 0.010. A similar examination of the data for Japan shows that the X ratio moved in the correct direction following six of the seven significant changes in the effective value of the yen during the period 1971 to 1981. In addition, the X ratio and the M ratio changed in the same direction on six of seven occasions. 'Significant' is defined here, as previously, to mean a movement of 5 per cent or more in the year over year effective exchange rates. If exports tend to move in the correct direction following an exchange-rate alteration, and if the import ratio tends to move in the same direction as the export ratio, then the overall trade balance can move in either direction. But this result suggests strongly that, via the export route, exchange-rate depreciations stimulate domestic production and, via income effects or whatever, they stimulate foreign production as well.

A complete model would have to examine the full range of complex relations involved — a freely floating rate will rise if, *ceteris paribus*, the trade balance increases, and the trade balance tends to increase if, *ceteris paribus*, the exchange rate falls. In addition, the lag structure and movements in the exchange rate that are not captured in the yearly averages are clearly important. However, for a large country in particular, such as the United States, it is important to realize that a fall in its exchange rate tends to promote economic activity at home and abroad, whereas a rise tends to depress economic activity at home and abroad. The tendency for imports to move in the same direction as exports following an exchange-rate revision suggests, among other possible explanations, that marginal import propensities are very high and that imports respond sharply to changes in income. This would be consistent with McKinnon's thesis that economies have become much more open, in 'goods' trade as well as in financial capital markets.

The analysis in Table 7.4 does not give much support to the thesis that the trade balance is dominated by the government sector account. If this relationship held, then the sign of the change in $(T - G)$ should be the same as the sign of the change in $(X - M)$. This is found to be so for two of the four cases in Canada, one of the two in Sweden, and one of the three cases in the United

States. (In two other cases in the United States, the change in the trade balance is zero.) For Britain, however, in five of six cases the change in $(T - G)$ has the same sign as the change in $(X - M)$. But too much significance cannot be placed on this, since changes in $(S - I)$ are generally also important in Britain. The search for a one-to-one relationship between changes in the government deficit and in the trade balance is not, in general, likely to be productive, since saving and investment decisions are simply going to be influenced by major internal or external shifts in demand.

In summary, signficant movements in exchange rates tend to be accompanied by changes in exports in the expected direction, and by changes in imports which parallel the changes in exports. Contrary to a common undergraduate error, an equal increase in exports and imports does not result in an unchanged GNP: imports are subtracted in calculating GNP, but only because they are included in the measures of C, I, G and X. The simple multiplier, in short, is unity under these conditions, not zero. However, the role of a large economy such as that of the United States needs to be examined more closely. Since an upward movement in the United States dollar, which tends to reduce United States exports and imports, is equivalent to a downward movement in the exchange rate of the rest of the world, why does this not result in increased exports and increased imports, thus offsetting the impact of the appreciation of the United States dollar? A possible but somewhat implausible reason is that a higher marginal propensity to import in the United States would give a net deflationary impact to the system as a whole. More realistically, the system can be viewed as a closed economy in which the real interest rate has been increased, so that the deflationary impact is the stronger one. This would be a straightforward Keynesian view. In monetarist terms, the matter is more complex, since the appreciation of the United States dollar, a key reserve currency, increases the real value of that component of foreign exchange reserves held in United States dollars, as well as the real value of United States dollar balances in general. This wealth effect might be expected to increase aggregate demand in the system. However, this effect will be reduced to the extent that an appreciation of the United States dollar is accompanied by a fall in the price of gold, since gold remains a very important component of foreign exchange reserves on a world-wide basis. There can, in practice, be little doubt that the run-up of world interest rates in the early 1980s, as a consequence of a restrictive United States monetary policy was, on balance, a deflationary influence on world aggregate demand.

BALANCE OF PAYMENTS POLICIES IN AN OPEC-CONSTRAINED WORLD

Coordination of Economic Policies

Despite the fact that both small and large countries are able, with a mixture of monetary, fiscal and exchange-rate policies, to expand aggregate demand in ways that have no, or limited, adverse balance of payments effects for themselves or for the world at large, it is obvious that concerted action by the industrialized countries would make the balance of payments problems arising from an expansionary policy much easier to manage. In particular, a simultaneous expansion of demand would, in principle, allow for equilibrium in the balance of payments with no exchange-rate movements, ignoring for the moment the crucial question of the probability of an increasing overall deficit with the OPEC nations, owing to increasing quantities of oil imports and to rising oil prices. Such coordination of policies could come from an IMF reformed to provide a world central banking function as envisaged by Keynes at Bretton Woods, or from an agreement among industrial countries to harmonize their aggregate demand policies. Unfortunately, neither solution seems probable. The IMF, with great difficulty, was able to agree to increase its lending powers in early 1983, but the United States and others provided strong resistance and would oppose any real expansion in IMF powers. The United States has shown that it will conduct whatever monetary policy is best for their economy in isolation, and has shown at the Versailles Conference of 1982 and elsewhere that it is not about to allow policy to be influenced to any significant degree by international considerations. Whether the world economy, with the United States, as odd-man-out, can develop a workable harmonious macroeconomic strategy is questionable, given the absence of any forceful leadership in this direction from Japan, Germany, France or Britain. However, it is also necessary to consider the question of a possible OPEC constraint on world economic recovery.

The Impact of OPEC

'An OPEC constrained world' is one in which petroleum supplies are effectively controlled by the OPEC cartel so that real oil prices are high with respect to historic levels, and real oil prices are volatile and unpredictable in the short run. The world was constrained in this sense from late 1973 to early 1983 at least, and despite some slight weakening of OPEC in early 1983, it is a clear possibility that the world will continue to experience such constraint throughout the 1980s. For OPEC one can also read Saudi Arabia, since Saudi Arabia has provided whatever control the cartel has possessed.

An OPEC constraint has two implications for the world economy, one 'real' and one 'monetary', but both actually and potentially very disturbing. On the 'real' side, there is a direct linkage between the amount of energy consumed and the level of real output, so that a cut-back or slow rate of growth of energy supplies, dictated by monopoly considerations respecting the price of oil, will cause a cut-back or slow down in real economic growth (see Begg, Cripps and Ward, 1981: 13–22). This 'quantity theory of energy' has obvious parallels to the 'quantity theory of money': energy times the coefficient of output/unit of energy input equals real output ($EA = Q$), as compared to the familiar $MV = PQ$. The energy equation has certain advantages over the money equation. It is easier to understand how E relates to Q than how M relates to P (or Q); A is probably more stable and predictable than V, and E can be more easily defined and has fewer close substitutes than M. According to the quantity theory of energy, real output can only be increased by increasing the coefficient of output per unit of energy input or by increasing energy supplies. High energy prices have tended and will tend to increase both A and E, at least for the medium term-horizon of 10–15 years. However, if high energy prices result from sharply reduced energy supplies owing to the actions of the cartel, real output will fall sharply before rising slowly. In addition, the recovery of real output will be hampered and perhaps halted by the OPEC balance-of-payments surplus engendered by high energy prices. Alternatively, a break-up of OPEC could lead to an increase in E and falling prices for energy, and therefore a fall in A. These questions are discussed more fully in later parts of the paper.

On the 'monetary' side, the arguments for a constraining effect from OPEC are more familiar. The OPEC countries as a group ran substantial balance-of-payments surpluses following 1973, surpluses which ranged as high as $100 billion per year. This means that the rest of the world had to run an equal-size deficit. Deficits of this order of magnitude among developed and non-oil-developing countries place severe strains on balance-of-payments adjustment mechanisms, and lead to high interest rates and restraint on growth in order to reduce the deficits. Interest rates have a dual role in depressing aggregate demand and hence imports, and in attracting foreign capital. Except to the extent that oil imports are reduced, however, these measures of constraint serve only to pass the deficit around from country to country like a hot potato, and to reduce output. Recycling of petro-dollars could in theory prevent these repercussions, as non-oil-producing countries borrow back OPEC's surpluses and continue to follow growth policies. In addition, OPEC surpluses have tended to fall as OPEC countries have increased their imports. Nevertheless, the overall effect of OPEC surpluses has been a deflationary one, as the 'taxes' paid by oil consumers to oil producers have resulted in an overall decline in aggregate demand. One reason for the failure of recycling to solve the balance-of-payments problem of the non-OPEC world arises because some countries have been able, despite OPEC, to run balance-of-trade surpluses. This has tended to push the adjustment burden on to the less flexible and adaptable countries, both developed and developing, and lenders not unnaturally will eventually become wary of lending billions of dollars to generally weak economies. Developing countries with exports concentrated in a few products are particularly vulnerable. Between 1974 and 1975 industrial countries as a group improved their balance-of-trade position by $37 billion, whereas non-oil-developing economies saw their balance of trade position worsen by $14 billion (IMF, *International Financial Statistics, Supplement on Trade Statistics, 1982*). This has been a common pattern.

Eliminating unemployment in an OPEC-constrained world is not easy, and may not even be possible. Expansion of aggregate demand tends to increase imports and increase already precarious trade deficits. Simultaneous demand-increases across a number of countries may tend to solve some of the problem of trade deficits by stimulating exports as well as imports for each country, but they bring the risk of a further tightening of the OPEC screw, a slow down in oil production and extremely high real oil prices perhaps as high as $100 per barrel of oil.

The 'Small'-Country Case

We look first at the position of a 'small' country in an OPEC-constrained world. For our purposes, a small country will be defined as one having no effect on prices, in terms of foreign currency, of either its exports or its imports (including oil), and no effect on its own real interest rate. Nominal interest rates will differ between countries, depending upon expectations of changes in exchange rates, which in turn are linked to differences in rates of inflation. The small country is thus 'open' to both trade and financial flows, but unable to influence the prices at which it will deal. Canada and Sweden would be examples. If we assume that the small country has an exchange-rate policy which is essentially a floating-rate policy, then fiscal policy will not provide an effective stimulus to aggregate demand. As Mundell showed, but as appears to be little understood among many policy-makers even after 20 years, in an economy with unemployment an expansion of government expenditure or a reduction in tax rates, holding the money stock constant, will result in an inflow of foreign capital, an appreciation of the exchange rate, and an equal and offsetting reduction in demand from declining exports and expanded imports (Mundell, 1968: chap. 18). Complete crowding out occurs even though the interest rate does not change. Fiscal policy is equally ineffective as a contractionary policy under these conditions, since reductions in government expenditure or increases in tax rates result in capital outflows (or smaller inflows), a depreciating exchange rate, and an increased trade surplus. These results will obviously be modified and somewhat muted by lags in the system and perhaps by induced changes in expectations and hence in real expenditure functions, but the general lesson is clear: one should not place much direct reliance on fiscal policy in a small country with a flexible exchange rate. However, fiscal policy could have a useful supplementary role, as will be seen when monetary policy is considered.

A small country with a flexible exchange rate wishing to expand aggregate demand can increase the domestic money supply, thus reducing the exchange rate and stimulating the trade balance. However, even a small country in an OPEC-constrained world may impose serious problems on others by reducing its imports and increasing its exports, since other countries will tend to be in a precarious balance-of-payments and unemployment position to begin with. Small countries wishing to avoid such beggar-my-neighbour policies might therefore seek to ensure that by-and-large their imports increase in line with their exports, as could be achieved by expansionary fiscal policy or tariff and quota reductions. This policy combination would seem to have political advantages over policy combinations which would expand aggregate demand internally and rely on tariffs or quotas to prevent a balance of payments problem from emerging as a result of increased imports. In a fixed-exchange-rate system a small country cannot influence exports directly and would thus tend to favour quotas or tariffs to prevent imports from increasing as a result of demand stimulation. This is an argument in favour of a flexible system. Under either system, an incomes policy will probably be required to prevent demand expansion from causing further increases in inflation rates.

The argument given above should not be interpreted too optimistically, for it is essentially an argument that a small country may, by a judicious mixture of policies, expand its output and employment in an OPEC constrained world. These policies will not solve the world's balance-of-payments problem, and indeed they will make these problems worse to the extent that the policies increase the demand for OPEC oil. These secondary efforts may well be unseen and hence ignored by the small country. In the pre-OPEC world, such considerations were not necessary since imports would tend to generate exports. In an OPEC-constrained world, imports tend to generate, in part, OPEC surpluses, and these surpluses do not automatically get recycled.

The 'Large'-Country Case

A 'large' country in an OPEC-constrained world, such as the United States, has a difficult problem to face, in that its actions can influence world interest rates and the price of oil. In 1981 and 1982 the United States solved the oil-price problem temporarily by causing such a sharp recession world wide that the price of oil fell in real terms and even in nominal terms. This is hardly a satisfactory solution for anyone. The recession was precipitated by the sharp increase in interest rates in the United States resulting from the Federal Reserve monetarist stance, an increase that led to a sharp increase in the price of the United States dollar in relation to European and Japanese currencies. The predictable result is a sharp balance of trade deficit in the United States, financed by a capital inflow.

The importance of being 'large' can perhaps best be seen by

comparing the United States and Canada with respect to the impact of a federal government deficit. In Canada, a federal deficit of the order of $20 billion, given flexible exchange rates and high capital mobility, can have virtually no real effect on the total level of demand in the economy because the deficit is financed by borrowing abroad. Since interest rates and real income are constant, saving and investment can be held constant, and under these conditions, $\Delta T - \Delta G = \Delta X - \Delta M$, where T = tax receipts, G = government expenditure, X = exports and M = imports. The relationship is derived from the familiar identity that $I + G + X = S + T + M$. In Canada, the federal government borrows relatively little in foreign markets directly, but provinces, municipalities and corporations are heavy foreign borrowers. In 1981, for example, Canada ran a current-account deficit of roughly $5 billion, purchased existing United States firms (mainly oil and real estate) in both Canada and the United States to a value of almost $12 billion, and added over $1 billion to foreign exchange reserves. This $18 billion financial requirement was financed by net long-term borrowing of about $13 billion and net short-term borrowing (including errors and omissions) of about $5 billion. For a comparison, in 1981, the federal government ran a fiscal deficit of $7.5 billion (Canada, *Economic Review 1982*, p. 102). In short, in a small country there is no real crowding out of overall expenditure from government deficits since those who cannot borrow at home simply borrow abroad. Alternatively, of course, expansionary fiscal policy can be viewed as raising the exchange rate and crowding out exports.

While Canada has been able to finance federal deficits of the order of $20 to $25 billion by foreign borrowing, no such option is available for the United States even though in relative terms its federal deficits are no larger: a $20 billion Canadian deficit is roughly equivalent to a $200 billion United States deficit, given the relative size of the two economies. There is simply no lender or group of lenders, OPEC in its heyday included, who can lend $200 billion per year to the United States, year after year. The inevitable result is that deficits of this order of magnitude are, given monetary restraint, accompanied by rising United States and world interest rates and by an appreciation of the United States dollar. Fiscal policy accompanied by monetary constraint crowds out domestic investment and exports through rising interest rates and rising exchange rates.

POLICIES TO DEAL WITH AN OPEC CONSTRAINT

The really significant question about a world economy unconstrained by OPEC is how to achieve such a situation. A fall in the price paid to OPEC for its oil would have positive worldwide effects on aggregate demand and on aggregate supply, in reverse manner to the impact of the OPEC tax increases of 1973 and 1979. Real GNP would rise, inflation would be abated, and industrial production, employment and profits would expand. For every Mexico with a deteriorating balance-of-payments situation, there would be three Brazils, Argentinas, and Indias whose balance of payments would improve. For every banker with a loan becoming soft, three bankers will find their customer's repayment possibilities increased. In 1979, the 30 developing countries with the largest foreign debts owed a total of $314 billion, about 30 per cent of which was owed by oil-producing countries (particularly Mexico and Venezuela). The 37 largest debtors among developing countries owed $310 billion to banks in mid 1981, of which $105 billion was owed by members of OPEC. To put these numbers into perspective, the accumulated balance-of-payments surplus of OPEC countries, over the period 1974 to 1982, equalled $458 billion.

The question, then, is how can non-OPEC countries avoid a situation where economic recovery is aborted by $100 per barrel oil and by a very large balance-of-payments surplus flowing to OPEC? Strategies to achieve this tend to fall into two groups, the direct and the indirect. The direct strategy is to cause a breakdown in OPEC such that OPEC will permanently lose its market power. The recession of the early 1980s does not qualify as a direct strategy since OPEC's diminished market power is attributed in large part to the, hopefully temporary, effects of the world-wide recession. Press reports suggest that about 30 per cent of the 12 million barrel per day cutback in output by OPEC members from 1981 to 1982 was attributable to the reduction in world demand, the rest being the result of a run-down of world oil stocks (30 per cent), the substitution away from oil as an energy source (25 per cent), and competition from non-OPEC sources (15 per cent). The indirect strategy is to generate non-OPEC energy sources so that dependence on OPEC supplies is broken. In brief, the direct strategy seeks to achieve low prices to oil producers and consumers, whereas the indirect strategy seeks to achieve low prices to OPEC producers, high prices to non-OPEC producers and high prices to consumers. Other things equal, the first is clearly superior to the second. The advantage of the direct method is simply, but importantly, the advantage of less scarcity (real or contrived). The disadvantage is that OPEC, even if broken, might rise again with renewed vigour. To prevent this, some substantial change in the world oil market would be required.

The most persuasive argument for change is one advanced by Adelman (1974), an argument that does not seem to have diminished in force over time. Simply put, Adelman's contention is that the cartel would be much more difficult to operate if the large multinational oil companies were not at least passively colluding by acting as 'tax-collecting agencies' for OPEC nations. Any effective cartel must control output and prevent price competition among members. A system of charging an indirect tax on the oil companies by the oil-producing countries sets an effective floor to the price of crude oil, which would not be there if the oil-producing countries themselves had to market the oil. If the producing countries had to sell the oil, the control of the market would be diminished. In Adelman's words:

Once they become 'formidable' buyers of crude oil rather than tax collecting agents, the market will look considerably different from what it does today. The oil companies are a big gun pointing towards the consuming countries, which ought to be pointed the other way. Hence, real nationalization is greatly to the advantage of the consuming countries.... The American government ought not to force American companies into being contractors, since they would merely be displaced by European or Asian companies. It must be done in unison or not at all. (Adelman, 1971: 64)

The direct strategy would thus depend upon a concerted approach by, say, the OECD nations, which prohibited their oil companies from owning any production or storage facilities outside the OECD nations themselves. As an indication of the hold that OPEC nations have over the multinational oil companies, the four major companies that have interests in Saudi Arabia were induced to buy crude oil from Saudi Arabia at the official $34 price to such a degree that in 1982 alone they lost $2.4 billion from having to purchase this higher-priced oil. Without this 'guaranteed' market, Saudi Arabia would have been much more receptive to a fall in the nominal price of oil. Also central to the direct strategy would be the necessity of preventing Saudi Arabia from having the dominant market share that effectively allowed the cartel to operate in the 1970s.

The indirect strategy of relying less on OPEC oil is based on the effect high oil prices will eventually have on reducing consumption by means of fuel-efficient conservation measures, and on increasing production from non-OPEC sources. The advantages of this over an OPEC-constrained world are that the energy coefficient will be reduced, the proportion of world output produced outside OPEC will be increased, and, with an appropriate optimal tariff strategy by consuming nations, the price paid to OPEC producers will be reduced. World output will be able to increase at a rate determined by the success of conservation efforts and of oil (and non-oil) exploration and development efforts, and would not be subject to OPEC's arbitrary production plans. The disadvantage of this strategy over the direct strategy is that high-cost energy is substituted for low-cost energy, and it is also vulnerable to the possibility that non-OPEC countries (Mexico, Britain, Canada?) might be induced to join OPEC, formally or informally, to increase their returns from oil.

Given the importance of the problem and the need for a solution if world economic growth is to be at acceptable rates, there is probably a case to be made for adopting both strategies. High oil prices resulting from taxes on consumers paid to the governments of those consumers are far less deflationary than taxes paid to foreign governments, and there are no negative balance-of-payments effects. However unlikely it is that OECD countries would effectively interfere in the operations of their oil companies, the pressure should be put in this direction, and not in giving assent to the view that a collapse of OPEC will result in the collapse of the economy world wide. As for the argument that an anti-OPEC policy would be viewed with dismay by third-world countries, seeing it as a put down by the rich of the poor, an effective counterargument would seem to be that economic growth will benefit developing as well as developed economies, and, conceivably, even OPEC countries. A recent Brookings study has stated that economic growth even in OPEC countries was faster in the decade preceding 1974 than in the years following 1974 (Fried, 1982: 11). As has been noted, the economy is like a bicycle, which, if operated too slowly, causes everyone to fall off. In addition, in relative terms, the adjustment burden generated by OPEC has fallen disproportionately on the third-world countries.

CONCLUSION

The implicit assumption of this paper is that economic recovery on any substantial scale will be accompanied by increased and perhaps escalating inflation, unless accompanied by a successful incomes policies. Even so, this substantial economic recovery will be thwarted, so long as OPEC remains strong, by sharp increases in the real price of oil and by slow or negligible increases in the world supply of energy. The result will be an OPEC-induced balance-of-payments constraint on world recovery. Some suggestions have been advanced as to how the OPEC problem might be resolved. Assuming that this can be achieved, prospects for strong, worldwide, economic growth depend upon the uncertain shoulders of the IMF or the United States, but, as pointed out above, neither the IMF nor the United States has the ability and the will to generate a coordinated and simultaneous expansion of world demand. Failing success in these directions, the paper suggests that small industrial countries have some limited freedom of action in terms of domestic exchange-rate policy to improve their own economic prospects, without indulging in or being accused of beggar-my-neighbour policies.

REFERENCES

Adelman, M. A. (1974) Politics, economics and world oil, *American Economic Review*, May.

Begg, I., Cripps, F. and Ward, T. (1981) The European Community: problems and prospects, *Cambridge Economic Policy Review*, December.

Chacholiades, M. (1978) *International Trade Theory and Policy*, New York: McGraw Hill.

Department of Finance, Canada, *Economic Review, April 1982*, Ministry of Supply and Service, Ottawa, 1982.

Fried, E. (1982) Energy security and the common interest, *The Brookings Review*, Winter.

Gordon, R. J. (1978) *Macroeconomics*, Boston: Little, Brown and Co.

Isard, P. (1977) How far can we push the 'Law of one price'?, *American Economic Review*, December.

International Monetary Fund, *International Financial Statistics, 1982 Yearbook*.

Kravis, I. B. and Lipsey, R. E. (1977) Export prices and the transmission of inflation, *American Economic Review*, February.

McKinnon, R. I. (1981) The exchange rate and macroeconomic policy: Changing postwar perceptions, *Journal of Economic Literature*, June.

Mundell, R. A. (1968) *International Economics*, New York: Macmillan.

8
The Implications of an Inflationary Bias
John Cornwall

INTRODUCTION

There are two basic questions in macroeconomic policy whose answers are critical for evaluating current economic policies. First, since in modern democracies there will be limits to how far and for how long the authorities may drive up the unemployment rates to reduce inflation, is it possible to bring down the rate of inflation to the desired level before some political constraint is encountered? The second question revolves around what is likely to happen if and when inflation rates are substantially reduced. Thus, assume that rates of inflation have been brought down to politically acceptable levels and either the authorities decide to restimulate the economy or the private sector experiences a sustained boom. Will inflation rates begin to accelerate when full employment is again realized or, worse, while involuntary unemployment is still substantial?

The experience of the last few years has provided an answer to the first question. Inflation rates have fallen dramatically in the OECD countries beginning in 1982. This has been accomplished by driving up unemployment rates, to double-digit levels in many countries, where they have remained since 1982. If Mrs Thatcher's electoral victory proves anything it is, that whatever political constraints there are on how high unemployment rates can rise, they are far less binding than most politicians and economists would have assumed as recently as only a few years ago. Inflation rates can be brought down in modern democracies by creating enough unemployment and governments need not fall.

---

* My thanks, once again, to Wendy Maclean for her comments and criticisms.

This recognition has been a source of mutual congratulation among governments, economists and central bankers in many countries. However, this is somewhat premature. For the critical test of restrictive aggregate demand policies as a cure for inflation is their long-run impact, when inflation has been wrung out of the system and, for whatever reason, the economy begins to expand. If such restimulation leads to accelerating inflation at full employment or even while unemployment remains high, the authorities must either choose to let inflation continue or they must choose to depress the economy again. In either case, policies like those which have been so widely adopted over the last decade must be considered a failure. Either they will have not been sufficient to cure inflation in the long-run or else they have only succeeded in doing so by creating secular, large-scale unemployment and stagnation.

Much use has been made by economists of the non-accelerating inflation rate of unemployment concept or NAIRU. Supposedly there is some unique rate of unemployment such that lower rates lead to accelerating rates of inflation and higher rates lead to deceleration. Without necessarily agreeing that there is any uniqueness to this rate, the second critical question just posed is whether at the rate of unemployment at which involuntary unemployment is zero, inflation rates accelerate. Is the full employment rate of unemployment the NAIRU?

Rather uncritically, large numbers of economists have taken to assuming that these two unemployment rates are the same. They do so by simply defining whatever unemployment rate turns out to be the NAIRU as the full employment rate. This is, at best, question begging. If they are not the same and rates of inflation tend to accelerate at full employment or when involuntary unemployment exists, then it will be said that modern capitalist economies suffer from an inflationary bias in a strong sense.

The position I would like to take in this paper is that an inflationary bias does exist in this sense. This bias is new to capitalism, having developed during the post-war period and can be traced primarily to developments in the labour market. In particular, what I would like to argue is that prolonged periods of full employment interact with unionization in such a way as to radically change the manner in which wages are determined. For accompanying full employment is a strengthening of the power of unions, due partly to the increased affluence of unions and partly to the development of the welfare state. As a result 'fairness considerations' come to dominate wage settlements. In addition a commitment to full employment together with the increased importance of non-price aspects of competition have worked to make employers more receptive to labour demands for fair wage settlements. Together these developments have radically altered labour markets and, in so doing, the inflationary process. The most important implication of this is that current restrictive policies will be seen to be a failure if and when an attempt is made to return to full employment. The next section discusses briefly certain institutional changes that have been important in changing the nature of inflation.[1]

THE CHANGING INSTITUTIONAL STRUCTURE

Consider a period before the Second World War in any one of today's modern capitalist economies. Trade unions exist but very likely the union movement is fragmented in the sense that collective bargaining is conducted between individual companies and their employed workers. Because we are considering a period before sustained full employment and the affluence it brings, unions would not yet have accumulated large financial resources for aiding their members during strikes and periods of unemployment, and unemployment insurance programmes would not have become common on a national scale. Taking into account these various considerations, it is most unlikely that labour markets would be integrated in the sense that wage decisions in one market were considered relevant for judging the fairness of wage settlements. Nor is it likely that changes in the cost of living would be an important consideration in settlements, even if reliable measures were available.

Instead, we would expect labour-market settlements to be dominated by the traditional economic forces of demand and supply (although certainly not the textbook forces of atomistic competition). Employers would be in a dominant bargaining position but it can be assumed that they would have to raise wages whenever labour markets tightened in order to fill the expanding number of vacancies. During periods of slack, they would not necessarily lower money wages absolutely in spite of their superior bargaining position, since workers' reaction to such behaviour might prove to be counter-productive. Rather a more rapid rate of increase of money wages during booms than recessions could be expected. In labour markets such as these, which characterize real-life labour markets in the OECD economies prior to the post Second World War period, rates of inflation of wages would more or less reflect the underlying state of the labour market, moving up and down with the business cycle.

It is important to note that in this world the inflationary process is very largely demand-pull and can be modelled using a comparative static framework. For example, as the economy expands and the demand for and supply of loanable funds increases, the rise in aggregate demand and the money supply will lead to tighter conditions in labour markets. Sooner or later shortages of labour will lead to wages being bid up. Successive increases in aggregate demand will continue to push up wages and if mark-up pricing is followed this will pass through to prices. But the important point to note is that there is a weak feedback from higher prices to wages as the cost of living figures little in wage settlements. As a result there is comparatively little in the way of dynamic lagged reactions involved in the inflationary process. As long as aggregate demand continues to grow, whether because of a rising money supply, increasing velocity, or both, inflation will persist. However, once the downturn comes, inflationary pressures will quickly slacken.

Consider now a world of affluent trade unions, endowed with large emergency funds, built up over the years of sustained prosperity, and a national system of unemployment insurance. Workers have more power relative to employers and can be expected to bargain more strongly in this full-employment world since they are better able to afford unemployment. They will therefore insist that their living standards be protected. By the same token, firms accustomed to full employment conditions rightly feel that rising labour costs can be passed through to prices without appreciable losses of sales. As a result, cost-of-living considerations will very much figure in wage settlements. In addition relative wages will be an important consideration. Instant and nationwide mass communication make workers aware of wage settlements elsewhere and full employment and affluence make such considerations enforceable in other wage settlements.

In these kinds of labour markets, traditional market forces of demand and supply would have a much less pronounced role to play in wage settlements. Fairness considerations, in which a fair wage settlement is defined in terms of the effect on real wages and the position of a labour group in the wage structure, would have a much more important weight.

THE 'NEW INFLATION'

The basis of cost-push inflation

Fairness considerations provide the rationale for what has come to be known as 'fix-price markets'. Fix-price markets are markets in which price changes (including wages) are little influenced by conditions of excess demand or supply but instead result from changes in 'costs' or unconventional forces, e.g. unit production costs in product markets and the cost of living and the wage structure in labour markets. In contrast, 'flex-price' markets are markets in which the familiar textbook demand and supply forces dominate.

Fix-price labour and product markets are the basic elements of two cost-push mechanisms, wage-price and wage-wage inflation, that have so transformed today's inflation. Wage-price inflation involves a process in which rising wages are passed through to prices as before, but now higher prices feedback to wages as workers demand and get real wage protection. Wage-wage inflation interacts with wage-price inflation but is a separate force in its own right. The process is simply one of wages in one market catching up with or leap-frogging wages elsewhere, significantly changing relative wages and giving rise to a perceived unfairness. Such feelings of 'relative deprivation' lead to wage demands elsewhere in order to reestablish the original 'fair' differentials. The process is intensified, the more fragmented and the less synchronized are collective bargaining arrangements within a country.

The two cost-push mechanisms reinforce one another and give inflation an impetus which is independent of the state of the economy over a range of unemployment rates. Thus, while both wage-price and wage-wage inflation are more intense at low unemployment rates than high, the influence of past events on current settlements increases in a cost-push world. For example, following a period of boom, unemployment rates may rise for some time before wage settlements are affected because of a felt need by labour groups to establish a fair real wage or a fair position in the wage structure.

Modelling inflation

The incorporation of the cost of living and of relative wages considerations into wages bargaining, justified by principles of fairness and enforceable under full employment by affluent unions, profoundly affects the nature of inflation. This is most apparent in considering the cost-of-living feedback effect. Before the post-war period, rising raw material prices and money wages would raise production costs and be passed through to prices. But without further stimulative demand impulses the inflationary process would not have an internal dynamic all its own. For example, a continuous growth of the money supply would be required to keep an inflationary gap open. There would be little feedback from the higher (and rising) prices to money wages during this process. As already pointed out, the inflationary mechanism can be adequately modelled within a comparative static framework. With feedback effects present, inflation can only be modelled within a dynamic framework that picks up the various lags and dynamic interactions. For example, if wage settlements are influenced by the rate of price inflation in the previous period, then an acceleration of wage inflation today is not merely passed through to prices. The rate of price inflation accelerates in the current period because of pass-through effects, but this will accelerate the rate of wage inflation in the next period and so on.

The impact of aggregate demand

However, even though wage settlements are strongly influenced by fairness considerations, changes in aggregate demand, as reflected in changes in the aggregate unemployment rate will also affect wage settlements. This comes not so much from shifting demand curves causing wages to be bid up or down in some kind of auction process as it does from the impact of labour market conditions on the relative strength of the two sides of the labour market. Thus, as unemployment rates fall labour bargains more forcefully and employers accede more readily to higher wage demands as labour can better face a strike and profit conditions are improving. This upward pressure on wage inflation would be present even if the labour movement was centralized in its bargaining. But to the extent that the labour movement is fragmented and bargaining decentralized, at lower unemployment rates the added aggressiveness of labour increases the frequency of disturbances of the relative wage structure. This leads to an intensification of the wage-wage as well as the wage-price inflationary processes.

The long-run and short-run Phillips curves

The presence of fairness considerations in wage bargaining, especially the feedback effect, points up the need to distinguish between the long-run and short-run Phillips curves. For example, if the rate of wage inflation depends upon the rate of price inflation in the previous period and the current unemployment rate, anything leading to a decline in unemployment will have a short-run effect on wage inflation. This can be treated as a movement along a short-run Phillips curve for wages. However, in the succeeding period there is a further increase in the rate of wage inflation even if unemployment rates do not change further. This comes about because of the pass-through impact of higher wages on prices in the initial period which then feeds back into wages in the succeeding period. But this has a further impact on price inflation, etc. Only when these dynamic interactions have worked themselves out and the rate of wage (and price) inflation stabilizes at a new higher rate is a second point on the long-run Phillips curve established.

As is easily shown more formally with mathematical models, an economy described by this kind of inflationary process has a long-run, steady-state, rate of wage (and price) inflation towards which it will converge in the absence of disturbances.[2] In the simple model just described this long-run rate of inflation will be a function of the rate of unemployment. However, such an economy will be subject to outside disturbances which activate the cost-push mechanisms. When this happens whatever long-run may have been realized will be disturbed. Depending upon the lagged structure and the parameters, these disturbances can lead to wide and prolonged deviations of the rate of inflation from the equilibrium rate (which depends upon the assumed fixed unemployment rate).

ASYMMETRIES

However, what has just been said implies that negative disturbances or a permanent increase in the rate of unemployment could lead to decelerating rates of inflation in exactly the same manner as positive disturbances or a permanent decrease in unemployment accelerate inflation rates. Unfortunately this is not the case, as sustained full employment in the presence of unionized labour also leads to important asymmetries. These give the inflationary bias to the system.

Recall Keynes's belief that money-wage levels respond in an asymmetrical way to excess demand and supply in labour markets. An excess demand for labour may well lead to money wages being bid up but an excess supply of labour due to inadequate effective demand would not see a fall in money wages. Rather a quantity adjustment in the form of increased unemployment would occur. Workers, keen to maintain their position in the wage structure would resist money-wage cuts because they could not be sure that other labour groups would be taking the same wage cut.

However, this view of labour markets continues to emphasize shifting demand-and-supply curves for labour as the chief determinant of changes in wages. What has just been said about wage determination in fix-price markets suggests focusing on the possibility of asymmetrical responses of workers to changes in the cost of living and changes in their position in the wage structure at any given unemployment rate. The issue is whether a decline in real wages or an unusually large wage increase somewhere that disturbs the wage structure will more likely or more strongly activate the wage-price and wage-wage mechanism upward as a rise in real wages or a relative wage decline somewhere will set off cumulative movements downward. The view adopted here is that there is an asymmetrical response to changes in these determinants of wage inflation just as there is to excess supplies and demands for labour. As a result there are additional reasons for the emergence of an inflationary bias than are given in *The General Theory*.

For example, a small wage increase, small relative to increases in the recent past or what was expected, in some 'key' sector of the labour market is not as likely to set in motion a competitive decline in wage increases, or at least one of anywhere near the same magnitude, as a relatively large wage increase would be to initiate a competitive rise in wage increases. Labour groups have much to gain if they respond strongly to large wage increases elsewhere, and they have little to gain by cutting back on wage demands when small wage increases take place in other markets.

Consider next the response to increases and decreases in the real wage (or to movements above or below their trend) at some given rate of unemployment. If the increase in the real wage is due to an unusually large increase in productivity or a favourable movement in the terms of trade, labour groups are not likely to reduce their money-wage claims, certainly not markedly. They will feel they deserve the unusual benefit. On the other hand, a decline in the real wage is more likely to be associated with an increase in money-wage demands, (or at least one greater in magnitude) than the decrease in money-wage demands is to be associated with an especially large real-wage increase. This is again because labour has little to lose and much to gain by this kind of forceful behaviour when real wages decline and little to gain by restraint when real wages rise. Note that relative wage considerations also strengthen this real-wage asymmetry. Individual labour groups will be reluctant to cut back on money-wage demands when real-wage increases have been unusually large because of their concern that they might fall behind in the wage structure.

The case against this asymmetry arises when collective bargaining is coordinated with macro policy goals, in which case the trade union leaders might be willing to cooperate and restrain their demands in the interest of some kind of long-run national goal. This is nothing more than introducing a kind of consensus incomes policy in order to make full employment and wage restraint consistent.

TWO KINDS OF INFLATIONARY BIAS

Bias in the weak sense

The static asymmetries just discussed lead immediately to an inflationary bias in the weak sense; the level of wages, and therefore of costs and prices, has a tendency to drift upward at full employment in the absence of additional policy measures to offset these movements, e.g. an incomes policy. This conclusion is reinforced by the likely upward trend of prices, again at full employment, in many commodity markets especially for food and energy. These latter trends arise from a tendency for the growth of demand to outstrip supply in conventional flex-price markets and from tendencies of governments to stabilize some commodity prices downward through stockpiling arrangements. This upward bias in wage and price levels is greatly magnified when certain dynamic considerations are taken into effect.

Bias in the strong sense

An inflationary bias in a strong sense is defined as a tendency for rates of wage and price inflation to move upward at full employment in the absence of additional policy measures. The presence of this bias is also made clear by concentrating on labour markets, but this time by studying the behaviour of wages over the business cycle.

Consider then a moderate business cycle in which booms and recessions are of approximately equal amplitude and duration with unemployment falling as much in the boom as it rises in the recession. In the early stages of the boom rising demand will have its first impact in markets for casual low-wage labour, the kind of labour markets that most resemble flex-price markets. Here money wages will rise both absolutely and relative to wages in fix-price labour markets. This leads to cost increases and a disequilibrium situation in which the relative wage structure has narrowed. Increasingly, as labour markets in general tighten, labour becomes more aggressive, employers less resistant to higher wage demands and the wage-wage inflationary process intensifies.

Pass-through effects from accelerated wage settlements ensure accelerated price inflation as well. Once price inflation gets into the system, the feedback effects keep the process going, especially so during the boom when employer resistance is at a minimum and unions deal from strength. As unemployment rates continue to fall up to the end of the boom, the whole process intensifies and wage and price inflation accelerate.

Once the downturn sets in, unemployment rates rise and a downward pressure on wage (and price) inflation develops because labour responds in a less aggressive manner in slack labour markets, and, other things being equal, disturbances to the wage structure become less frequent. But other things will not be equal in the recession. The extent to which wage structure is disturbed is both a function of the unemployment rate and also of the past history of disturbances. In particular, the tendency for the wage structure to narrow during the boom in the manner just described sets in motion delayed adjustments. These are such that wage-wage inflationary forces will not die out as rapidly as they intensified during the boom. The ability of more powerful labour groups to widen the dispersion of the wage structure during the recession, a dispersion that narrowed during the previous boom will lead to this. They will not be deterred by the reduction of wage settlements elsewhere.

Consider the real wage influence. Synchronized booms have generated rapid increases in prices in international commodity markets leading to a movement of the terms of trade against the importing country and to a decline in real wage growth. If this occurs just before the recession, pressure will mount up to protect real wages through accelerated money wage settlements during the slump. The cyclical decline in productivity during recessions similarly works to reduce real wage growth. In both cases the desire to resist real wage cuts will work to offset the dampening influence of higher unemployment on money wage demands.

The result of these influences is that wage inflation accelerates more rapidly during the boom than it decelerates during a recession of comparable amplitude and duration. Rates of price inflation over the cycle will depend upon the behaviour of wages and productivity. Typically, the rate of growth of labour productivity has a pronounced procyclical pattern, rising sharply during the boom (along with the rate of wage inflation) and falling sharply during the recession (while wage inflation rates fall proportionately less). The result is that the decline in the rate of growth of labour costs during the slump is even less evident than that of wage inflation and may be non-existent. This acts to maintain the rate of price inflation during the slump which, because of feedback effects, acts to maintain wage inflation.

The net effect of these influences during mild recessions and booms is to cause inflation rates to ratchet upwards. This assumes cycle phases of similar amplitude and duration. Once a policy response is introduced, the impact of an inflationary bias in the strong sense can be phrased differently.

1. It takes longer through restrictive demand policies to reduce the rate of inflation than it does to increase the rate of inflation by an equal amount through expansionary policies.
2. From cycle-to-cycle inflationary rates ratchet upwards unless policy-induced periods of recession are increasingly substituted for those of low unemployment.
3. High and accelerating rates of inflation are easier to get into a system than they are to get out. The cost-push mechanism work to transform the static asymmetries into dynamic ones and make inflation rates very unstable upwards at full employment.

WHY INFLATION RATES FELL BUT FELL SLOWLY

Since fix-price labour markets are based on fairness considerations, considerations that have arisen primarily because of unions interacting with full employment and affluence, a clearer explanation of the recent decline in inflation rates emerges. The inflation part of stagflation can always be eliminated if unemployment is allowed to rise and remain high until the kinds of safety nets we associate with affluence have been removed. What is involved is to so increase unemployment that wage settlements are no longer largely framed in terms of a fair real wage and a fair relative wage. Once this happens a 'take it or leave it' attitude on the part of employers will dominate wage settlements. In the interim, inflation rates may be slow to come down because fairness considerations still dominate over fear of unemployment. The latter becomes overwhelming when unemployment rates have become high enough to affect the primary labour force, i.e. male workers with seniority.

This is the explanation suggested by events of the 1970s. Following the boom of the early 1970s throughout the OECD, a recession set in almost everywhere by 1974. For the first time in the post-war period the policy response was one of allowing and even encouraging the recession to develop because of the overwhelming fear by the monetary and fiscal authorities that the recent inflation had gotten out of hand. From 1974 to 1976 inflation rates fell markedly in many countries, but throughout the remainder of 1970s they levelled off at a rate appreciably above that of the 1950s and early 1960s.

The drastic decline in inflation from 1974 to 1976 can be attributed to a large extent to the rapid (but short-run) decline in international commodity prices and prices of foodstuffs and the feedback effect of this on wages. The failure of wage and price inflation to fall further after 1976 is well explained along the lines just suggested. In most all the OECD countries real wages failed to grow at rates similar to those of the 1950s and 1960s, partly because of the slowdown in productivity growth and partly because of adverse movements in the terms of trade. In many countries such as Sweden wage-wage inflation was a problem of some concern. At the same time unemployment, while high compared to the 1950s and 1960s, was low compared to what it was about to become in the 1980s.

Inflation rates accelerated at the beginning of the 1980 due largely to the run of oil prices interacting with the kinds of dynamic processes already described. Only by 1982 do inflation rates in most countries begin to come down to levels considered satisfactory by the authorities. But by 1982 unemployment rates had also reached unprecendented post-war highs everywhere. Members of the primary labour force were now facing layoffs for the first time on a wide scale. When this occurs fairness considerations no longer dominate wage settlements as seen by the willingness of labour to accept take it or leave it offers. In this respect labour markets resembled those of the nineteenth century by 1982. The costs of reducing inflation are notably large.

THE CREDIBILITY HYPOTHESIS

Following almost a decade of high unemployment, the predicted unemployment for the OECD countries in 1984 is put at 35 million. It has been argued by some, especially the monetarists, that this unemployment is not as serious a welfare problem as the numbers suggest. Unemployment according to this view is largely voluntary and reflects 'search activity' or a 'rational quest for self improvement'. My concern here is not with the unreality of this belief but with another argument, also advanced by economists who believe in the value of restrictive policies for curing inflation. I refer here to those who believe that if restrictive policies are properly constructed and applied, they can permanently bring down inflation rates and they can do so quickly and with little cost in terms of unemployment, whether the latter is considered voluntary or not. Improper formulation and implementation of restrictive policies in the recent period can account for the large costs of policy according to this view.

More specifically, advocates of what has come to be known as the Credibility Hypothesis (CH) argue that in order for restrictive policies to work properly it is necessary for the authorities to convince the right groups that, (a) there is no alternative way in which to get rid of inflation, and (b) the authorities will adhere to restrictive policies until inflation has indeed been eliminated.[3] The way to achieve credibility is to so sharply apply restrictive policies that the size of the policy shock will alter expectations in the intended direction. If this is done properly then inflation will die out rapidly and we can be transported back to the golden age of the 1950s and early 1960s.

In evaluating this argument it should be noted at the outset that most of the discussion has focused on bringing inflation down and little has been said about returning to full employment subsequently without reigniting the inflation. Thus, the two basic questions raised at the beginning are very much involved here. First a modification of the question posed there, is it possible to bring down inflation quickly with low unemployment costs? Second, assuming that this can be done, is it then possible to restimulate the economy and return to full employment without causing inflation rates to again accelerate? Note again that even if the answer to the first question were yes but the answer to the second question is no, current restrictive policies must be judged a failure. They have not been sufficient to permanently eliminate inflation.

With regard to the first question it is true that in countries like Japan inflation rates were brought down between 1974 and 1978 from 24.3 to 3.8 per cent with only a small cost in terms of unemployment; the unemployment rate rose from 1.4 to 2.2 per cent from 1974 to 1978.[4] But the Japanese success is exceptional. Moreover, the Japanese trade unions and employers have traditionally conducted wage negotiations with a deep concern that they be in harmony with national objectives such as price competitiveness. In other words, the success in bringing down inflation in Japan is better attributed to the success of a voluntary incomes policy.

Only in the English-speaking countries might it be said that there has been some sort of test of the CH. In these countries, unlike Japan and most of Continental Europe, when restrictive policies have been used, they have usually been the sole anti-inflationary instrument of policy. Here the issue is anything but clear cut. In these countries the process of squeezing inflation out of the system has and continues to be long and painful so much so that this can be offered as evidence against the CH. On the other hand, believers in the CH can and have argued that restrictive policies were never made credible or, if they were, not until very recently.

FEAR AS AN INCOMES POLICY

However, this part of the issue of evaluating the effectiveness of past or future policies can be circumvented. The true test of the merit of restrictive policies, those based on the CH included, is what happens if an attempt is made after eliminating inflation to return to full employment.

The answer given by advocates of current policies to all this is that capital and labour will have learned their lesson over the past decade and will come to realize that if wage and price setting is not carried out in the national interest, the authorities will again apply restrictive policies. Recognizing this, wages and prices will be determined in a manner consistent with zero or low rates of inflation.

Now it is important that everyone be clear about just what is being argued here. What is to come out of a period of hardship and the induced fear of possible future hardships is the coordination of collective bargaining and price setting with the national goals of wage restraint and price stability on a voluntary basis, in other words a successful, long-run voluntary incomes policy. This is a novel and startling addition to a class of incomes policies that may be termed consensus incomes policies. These seek compliance with wage and price norms through measures that induce capital and labour to internalize the costs of their price and wage behaviour. 'Jaw-boning', tripartite arrangements and now fear all qualify as special types of voluntary, consensus incomes policies.

The coordination of collective bargaining and price decisions with national goals in such a way that wage and price restraint is forthcoming has been tried with various degrees of success throughout the post-war period. A realization that the underlying inflationary mechanism is inherently explosive underlies the use of such policies. It has been most noticeably successful in Japan but many Continental countries have also achieved a good deal of success with such policies. Consensus policies have met with little success in the English-speaking countries. Such policies should be contrasted with the purely statutory wage and price controls as well and with 'incentives policies' such as a tax-based incomes policy (TIP) that work indirectly to achieve compliance through a system of financial rewards and penalties.

The countries in which consensus incomes policies have been most successful, Japan and some Continental economies, differ widely in their institutions, traditions and histories, but have one thing in common, the industrial relations system (IRS) can be described as cooperative. Whether industrial relations are adversarial or cooperative is clearly a matter of degree but it is useful to think of two pure types. On the one hand, with an adversarial IRS, a 'we' versus 'them' attitude is taken by management and labour, trust is absent and conflict often encouraged. On the other hand, a cooperative IRS stresses a unity of purpose and seeks to identify and strengthen areas of common interest; it attempts to build trust and downplay conflict and stresses sharing economic success. The near bi-modal distribution of strike records of the OECD economies in the post-war period suggests a dichotomy of industrial-relations systems in affluent economies may not be too far from the mark.

Believers in the long-run worth of restrictive policies would have us believe that the potentially unstable inflationary mechanism can be contained by substituting a policy of fear for one based on trust, cooperation and shared long-term benefit.

WHAT HAPPENS WHEN WE REFLATE?

It is helpful in analysing this view to concentrate on the likely response of the trade unions to a restimulation of the economy. Consider first the English-speaking economies, in which the belief in restrictive policies as a permanent cure for inflation has been strongest and in which industrial relations are the most conflict-ridden. These are also the countries in which labour has felt that it has been the prime target of restrictive policies in the current period.

Stimulative policies are now to be introduced following a period of policy-induced high unemployment. What is at issue is whether, as labour markets tighten, labour will have learned its lesson, whether the fear of future unemployment will keep labour from formulating wage demands in terms of fairness considerations.

It is my view that all the earlier arguments that inflation rates tend to accelerate at full employment (in the absence of an incomes policy) are strengthened. When unemployment rates fall during a boom, inflation rates begin to rise. By the time full employment has been realized, there is no reason to believe that cost-push forces and positive disturbances will not once again set in motion unacceptable rates of inflation. But outside disturbances activate the cost-push mechanisms upward at any rate of unemployment at which fairness considerations influence wage bargaining. Thus even if stimulative policies have not yet brought the economy back to full employment, as long as unemployment has been reduced enough to bring into play the wage-price and wage-wage mechanisms, there will be a tendency for inflation rates to be unstable upwards. The behaviour of inflation during the period from 1976–9 suggests this might take place at rather high rates of unemployment.

However, there will be an additional force at work that was not present before the restrictive policies of the 1970s; and that is that the lessons labour will have learned over the past decade are that they have been the chief victims of restrictive policies and that, as their market power rises with the employment rate, they have a chance to recoup their past losses. Efforts will be made to recapture real-wage losses through accelerated wage settlements. Especially strong efforts will also be made to restore the 'correct' wage structure in the only way possible. One very important institutional characteristic of the labour movement in English-speaking countries is decentralized decision-making in collective bargaining. Wage-wage inflation especially will intensify with a decentralized labour movement, since no group can be sure that the many other labour groups are so struck with fear that they will not be doing so.

In countries like France and Italy with more centralized decision-making but adversarial IRS, similar results will be forthcoming. Wage-wage inflation may be less of a problem but past antagonisms towards policies undertaken without consultation with the unions will only lead labour to demand that employers bear most of the cost of policies during this period.

Only in countries in which a tradition of consultation with the trade unions and a long history of cooperation between capital and labour as well as government has been established could we expect wage restraint as unemployment rates fall. But success here is not so much a matter of fear. It will be the result of the belief that the costs of past periods of restraint were shared by all. For example, labour will feel that past restrictive policies were not undertaken to reduce labour's power but rather in response to payments difficulties induced by OPEC.

THE ALTERNATIVE TO ECONOMIC DECLINE

The implications of an inflationary bias are serious for all countries. For the English-speaking countries it means that even without a balance of payments constraint, stimulative policies by themselves are not sufficient to return to full employment without inflation. Past periods of policy-induced recessions do not permanently cure inflation unless, of course, high unemployment rates are maintained indefinitely. If anything they intensify inflationary pressures at full employment in the absence of an incomes policy. The same is true for an other economy characterized by adversarial industrial relations.

On this reading the alternatives available to the various countries are threefold. First, the stimulative policies can be reintroduced without additional measures for dealing with the impact of such policies on wages and prices. As the economy moves toward full employment there will be a positive impact on productivity growth but inflation rates can be expected to accelerate and payments problems may well develop. Secondly, stimulative policies can be introduced cautiously to see how far unemployment can be reduced before inflation rates accelerate. With an inflationary bias this policy will sooner or later have to be reversed. If it can be assumed that productivity growth is negatively related to the rate of unemployment, the view taken here, the long-run effects of this policy will be relatively mild inflation but stagnation. Of course, if governments fear inflation enough, they may never restimulate the economy in which case this option is simply 'stagnation without inflation'.[5] Thirdly, some form of permanent incomes policy can be adopted in an effort to coordinate collective bargaining with the goals of stable prices at full employment. If successful, growth will resume as well and stagflation will come to an end.

However, the first alternative of 'growth with inflation' is really not politically feasible. It is difficult to think of the monetary and fiscal authorities in any of the modern capitalist economies pursuing full employment policies without regard to their inflationary impact. The adverse effect of such policies on inflation rates would generate a strong reaction even in a closed economy. In an open economy such policies would also lead to a 'currency crisis', with widespread speculation against the currency.

If economic decline is measured in terms of little or zero growth, then of the three alternatives the only politically feasible one to decline is the implementation of a permanent incomes policy at the same time as aggregate demand policies are used to move the economy back to full employment.

Whether or not such a policy can be made to work is another matter. But in this regard the economist is in a position to be of some help. He can publicize a new set of credibility conditions to be substituted for those formulated by advocates of restrictive policies. Instead of supporting policies of firm resolve to bring down wages and prices through what the authorities (incorrectly) believe to be the only means available, i.e. restrictive aggregate demand policies, economists can foster acceptance of the correct credibility conditions. And these are that what influential economic groups must recognize is that (a) because of a permanent inflationary bias, there is no alternative to a permanent incomes policy for achieving wage and price stability at full employment; and (b) if an incomes policy cannot be made to work, the authorities will reinstate restrictive demand conditions thereby guaranteeing continuous stagnation and economic decline.

Once these two conditions are met an incomes policy can be said to be credible and the first step will have been taken to end inflation and ultimately stagnation. The first condition reveals one of the most important implications of an inflationary bias. Inflation cannot be permanently removed from a full employment capitalist system by restrictive aggregate-demand policies. Such policies are not a sufficient condition for the eventual return to full employment without inflation. A permanent incomes policy is a necessary condition for ending stagflation. The second condition recognizes that government and national and international financial bodies (such as the IMF) are so concerned about inflation that they will never seriously accept full employment as a possible or even desirous policy goal unless they can be sure that it is under control. The use of incomes policies is necessary to allay these fears. Without such a policy, governments will choose a policy of stagnation without inflation.

INFLATION IS ALWAYS AND EVERYWHERE A POLITICAL PHENOMENON

The possibility of a workable incomes policy means that restrictive aggregate demand policies may not be even necessary for ending stagflation. However, there still remains the issue of what kind of incomes policy is appropriate for any country and what additional conditions must be met before such policies will be successful. Clearly the success of any government intervention in the form of an incomes policy is most importantly dependent upon the quality of government leadership. A government must be able to articulate and administer a programme that is widely accepted before any kind of incomes policy can succeed. To rephrase the whole argument, if price and wage stability cannot be realized and maintained without greater government intervention and on a permanent basis, then inflation is always and everywhere a political phenomenon. And if the achievement of full employment, and the induced productivity growth associated with a return to full employment, depends upon containing inflation then unemployment and stagnation are ultimately political phenomena. Contrary to the popular notions circulating today, more not less government intervention is required if capitalist economies are again to function properly. But this is merely to rephrase the implication of an inflationary bias just cited.

What comes out of all this is a simple but basic point and that is that far from being self-regulating, capitalism is constantly creating new problems for itself that must be tackled in order to prevent a serious malfunctioning. Rising per capita incomes are the catalyst. As Keynes noted half a century ago, affluence leads to problems of effective demand. Discretionary intervention or 'activism' by governments is then necessary. Sustained and increasing affluence fostered by a prolonged period of full employment such as the 1950s and 1960s leads to an inflationary bias. Further government intervention to deal with an even more difficult problem is now required to prevent economic breakdown.

Another implication of an inflationary bias is that strong, intelligent, conciliatory political leadership is required to end stagflation.

THE NEED FOR INTERNATIONAL COORDINATION

Once the closed economy assumption is dropped the only alternative to economic decline becomes highly conditional. Given the present international monetary arrangements and given the high degree of economic interdependence between countries, any country attempting to move to full employment is most likely to encounter serious difficulties even if initially there is wide acceptance of an incomes policy. For a restimulation will likely lead to a serious balance-of-payments deficit and speculation against the currency. If the currency is allowed to depreciate, this is likely to lead to an importation of inflation and an undermining of the incomes policy that was initially accepted. If attempts are made to limit the depreciation, adjustments may have to be made through an induced decline in imports, i.e. the full-employment goal will be sacrificed through a sharp reversal of the now stimulative aggregate demand policy.

This suggests, at the very least, the need for a large number of countries to coordinate their policies so that the 'leakages' into imports for each country pursuing expansionary policies are offset to the maximum extent possible by rising exports. In addition, a coordinated expansionary policy must be accompanied by measures that prevent this expansion from driving up prices in international commodity markets. This includes the market for oil. In short, what is needed is nothing less than development of a new international order which can lead to external as well as internal (full employment with stable prices) balance in the various countries.

It is hard to be anything but pessimistic about the alternatives to economic decline. For the time being, there seem to be none.

NOTES

1. This section relies heavily on Lewis, W. A. (1978) *Growth and Fluctuations: 1870–1913*, George Allen & Unwin: London; Phelps Brown, E. (1968) *A Century of Pay*, Macmillan: London; Phelps-Brown, E. (1971) The analysis of wage movements under full employment, *Scottish Journal of Political Economy*, November; Scitovsky, T. (1978) Market power and inflation, *Economica*, August.
2. The general class of inflation models being considered here are those in which the rates of price and wage inflation are treated as a distributed lag function of current and past rates of wage and price inflation, respectively, and unemployment. Additional explanatory variables can be considered provided they are predetermined. Given some values for all the predetermined variables, some restrictions on the form of the equations, a two-equation system of difference equations is sufficient to derive the long-run rates of wage and price inflation.
3. See Fellner, W. (1980) The valid core of the rationality hypothesis in the theory of expectations, *Journal of Money, Credit and Banking*, November.
4. The inflation data is found in IMF, *International Financial Statistics, Supplement in Price Adjustment*, 1981 and November, 1982. The unemployment figures are taken from OECD, *Economic Outlook*, Paris, December, 1982, Table R12.
5. Destroying the union movement is not an alternative in a democracy. They will rise up again under full employment conditions.

AUTHOR INDEX

Addison, J. T., 127n
Adelman, M., 154
Akerlof, G. A., 119n
Altonji, J. G., 119n
Begg, I., 148n
Baily, Martin, 37
Barro, R. J., 118n
Blinder, Alan, 42, 68
Bouey, Gerald K., 114n
Brittan, Leon, 74
Buiter, Willem, 68
Chacholiades, M., 136n
Clark, K. B., 116n, 119
Cobbett, William, 71
Cornwall, John, 14, 17, 18
Courchene, T., 56–57
Cripps, Francis, 74, 148n
Disraeli, Benjamin, 71
Eckstein, Otto, 45
Ettlin, Franz, 96
Feldstein, M. S., 113n, 117n
Fellner, W., 177n
Freeman, R. B., 119, 119n, 125n
Freidman, Milton, 48, 116, 121
Fried, E., 155n
Galbraith, John Kenneth, 30
Gilmour, I., 71n
Godley, Wynne, 13, 16, 20
Gordon, Robert, J., 136n
Gray, M., 52
Hall, R. E., 119n
Hayes, J., 126n
Hicks, J. R., 67
Hirschmann, Albert O., 123
Hume, David, 133
Isard, P., 134n
Johnson, Lyndon B., 26
Kerr, C., 115n
Keynes, John M., 8, 62, 64, 70–72, 76,
    77, 78, 82, 101, 147, 164, 176
Kimball, L. J., 120

Kravis, I. B., 134n
Laidler, David, 114, 125
Lerner, Abba, 38
Lewis, W. A., 177n
Lindbeck, Assar, 100
Lipsey, Richard, 13, 14, 16, 52, 120, 134n
Lucas, R., 117n
Lundberg, Eric, 13, 14, 15, 16, 17
Marx, Karl, 39
McKinnon, R. I., 139–145
Medoff, J. L., 119n
Mitchell, Daniel, 34
Mitchell, P. J. B., 120n
Mitterand, F., 102
Mundell, R., 133, 150
Nixon, Richard M., 26, 132
Nordhaus, W. D., 113
Nutman, P., 126n
Okun, A. M., 38, 113, 114,
Osberg, Lars, 14, 15
Ostry Sylvia, 115n
Phelps Brown, E., 177n
Phelps, E. S., 116
Rapping, L., 117n
Reagan, Ronald, 30
Reynolds, Lloyd, 115n
Schumpeter, J., 104
Scitovsky, T., 177n
Sinclair, Alasdair, 14, 16, 17
Siebert, W. S., 127n
Solow, R. M., 120
Summers L. H., 116n, 119
Thatcher, Margaret, 20, 23, 30, 50, 157
Tobin, James, 14, 15, 16, 18, 45, 68, 113
Volcker, Paul, 20
Wallich, H., 38
Ward, T., 148n
Weintraub, S., 38
Wicksell, Knut, 95
Wilberforce, William, 95
Woods, H. D., 115n

SUBJECT INDEX

aggregate demand
   assymetric impact, 8
   and exchange rates, 138, 147
   and interest rates, 149
   policies, 16–17, 146, 147, 175, 177
   restriction of, 3, 12, 17, 158
   and wage rates, 160, 162
anti-inflation policies, 42, 48, 113, 118
Argentina, 153
Austria, 35

balance of payments
   constraint, 2, 17, 83, 132–3, 174
   deficit, 17, 75, 87, 94, 99, 147–8, 153, 176
   equilibrium, 106–7, 147
   surplus, 134, 148–9
bankruptcy, 22, 35
Bank of Canada, 15, 41, 43–5, 47–9, 56
Brandt Commission, 107
Brazil, 153
Bretton Woods, 94, 132, 147

Canada
   collective bargaining, 49
   deficit, 46, 152
   exchange rate, 45, 137, 143
   inflation rate, 43, 44
   macroeconomic policy, 43
   monetary gradualism, 43–4, 47
   monetary growth rate, 43
   wage and price controls, 43, 50
   wage setting, 31, 43
   unemployment, 50
capitalism, 1, 5, 7, 10, 16, 39
central bank credibility, 11, 16, 24, 25, 26, 58, 118, 123
collective bargaining
   centralized, 31–2, 173
   decentralized, 31–2, 159, 162, 173
   and macroeconomic goals, 17, 165, 171
   synchronized, 32, 161
   unsynchronized, 48
commodity
   arbitrage, 134–5
   markets, 9, 27, 121, 165
   prices, 33, 73, 77, 165, 168
Consumer Price Index (CPI), 33, 43
credibility hypothesis, 169–70
cycles, 29, 32, 121, 160, 166, 167

Davis–Bacon Act, 36
debt
   bank, 79
   LDC, 153
   international, 22, 88
   private, 79–80
   public, 79–86
depression, 35, 66
disinflation, 20, 21, 24, 25, 29, 39, 73, 119
domestic absorption, 135, 139

EFO model, 17, 94–8
elasticities, 100, 104, 135, 142
European
   exchange rates, 45
   inflation rates, 20
   interest rates, 45
   wage rates, 31, 32, 42
European Economic Community (EEC), 75
exchange controls, 137
exchange rates
   appreciation of, 150
   depreciation of, 16, 77, 97, 104, 177
   devaluation of, 98, 134–5, 137–8, 139–43
   effective, 140
   fixed, 104, 133
   flexible (floating), 75, 134, 145, 150–1
   in UK, 75

expectations
  exchange rate, 150
  inflationary, 6–8, 9, 28–9, 39, 113, 118, 119, 120
  profit, 87
  rational, 48, 118
  wage, 48–9
expenditure switching, 135
export
  expansion, 105
  ratios, 143–4
  subsidies, 87

Federal Reserve, 25, 26, 41, 43
fiscal policy, 26, 38, 64, 68–69, 73, 74–5, 79, 106, 117, 118, 147, 152

gain-sharing, 34
General Agreement in Tariffs and Trade (GATT), 46, 76, 136
General Theory, The, 67, 78, 101, 164
gradualism, 15, 47
Great Depression, 25, 41, 115, 126
Gross National Product (GNP)
  gap, 58
  growth, 23, 24, 89, 101
growth
  balanced, 87, 91, 109
  constraints to, 64, 89
  export-led, 88
  of energy supplies, 148
  of trade, 88, 104–5
  world economic, 110, 155

imbalances
  external, 16
  in LDCs, 88
  national, 88
  structural, 87
import
  prices, 75
  propensity, 76, 143, 145
  restrictions, 88
  substitution, 104, 105
income
  family, 113, 119
  distribution, 101
  national, 67, 78–9, 82
  real, 63, 75, 126
incomes policies
  consensus, 17, 104, 171, 176
  costs of, 38
  permanent, 10, 17, 174–5
  tax-based, 38, 133, 171
  voluntary, 29, 32, 38, 136, 170, 171
indexation, 33, 143
India, 153

industrial policy, 87
industrial relations, 170, 173
inflation
  accelerating, 1, 7, 9, 10, 13, 15, 16, 17, 41, 46, 55–6, 66, 77, 113, 121, 158, 162, 166, 167
  accountancy, 82–3
  anticipated, 113
  causes, 27, 28, 35, 42–3
  constraint, 83
  cost-push, 8–10, 35, 161–2
  costs, 14, 42, 45, 59, 112–13, 169
  demand-pull, 6, 13, 160
  double digit, 20, 51, 70
  expectations of, 6–8, 15, 28, 39, 42–3, 52, 113, 119, 121
  rates, 4–5, 10, 20, 42–3, 45, 50, 63, 87, 88, 93, 104, 111, 168
  secular, 51, 55
  structural, 38
  wage and price, 4–5, 14, 115, 166
  wage-price, 161–2, 173
  wage-push, 35, 51, 73
inflationary bias, 10–11, 15, 17, 29, 52, 158, 164, 165–6, 167, 173, 175, 176
interest rates, 24, 41, 46, 47, 57, 75, 87, 106, 122, 150
International Monetary Fund (IMF), 70, 137, 147, 156, 175
investment, 16, 53, 67, 87, 101, 102
Israel, 136

Japan
  exchange rate, 145
  gain-sharing, 34
  inflation rates, 2, 170
  macroeconomic policies, 20, 171
job vacancy rate, 27, 37, 96, 121

Labour
  contracts, 32, 48, 119–20
  costs, 97
  economics, 112, 115–18, 121
  expectations, 48
  markets, 14, 37, 93–94, 112, 114, 118, 121, 124, 127, 159–60, 164–5
  mobility, 15, 124–5
  productivity, 95, 167
  supply, 118
laisser faire, 72, 77
Less Developed Countries (LDCs), 88, 107

Macroeconomic
  instruments, 76
  models, 120
  strategy, 147

Subject Index

macroeconomic policy
 expansionary, 8, 27, 117, 172–3
 Keynesian, 67
 post-war, 63–5, 73
 restrictive, 1–2, 9, 10–11, 14, 27, 30, 105, 169–70, 172–3
manpower policies, 37
marketing boards, 54
McCracken gap, 90
Mexico, 153
monetarism, 6–8, 11, 24–6, 30, 41–3, 50, 56, 58, 65, 69, 73–4, 91, 102, 106, 146, 169
monetary
 expansion, 50
 gradualism, 43–44, 47
 growth, 44
 targets, 44, 48, 90, 56–7, 74, 119
monetary policy
 and inflation, 7, 50, 69
 restrictive, 45, 47, 49, 55, 69, 80, 87, 106, 107, 139, 146
 stimulative, 16, 69, 106, 117
money
 demand, 25, 31, 44, 57
 supply, 7, 9, 12, 44, 48, 50, 90, 118
 reserve base, 48
 velocity of, 43, 44, 48
monopoly power, 8, 35, 70
multiplier, 67, 79, 80, 146

NAIRU (Non-Accelerating Inflation Rate of Unemployment), 11, 15, 16, 26, 27, 29, 31, 34, 36, 37, 53, 118, 121, 158
neoclassical economics, 6, 59, 102
North American
 inflation, 20
 unemployment, 23
 wages, 31, 32

oil prices, 16, 23, 27, 73, 147, 148, 153–4, 155, 169
Organization for Economic Cooperation and Development (OECD), 1–2, 10, 112, 136, 154, 157, 160, 168, 169, 172
Organization of Petroleum Exporting Countries (OPEC), 9, 14, 17, 106–7, 173

Phillips Curve, 37, 89, 96, 118, 163
post-Keynesian economics, 10–11, 12–13, 29
prices
 agricultural, 37, 42
 asymmetrical behaviour of, 29, 31, 37, 42
 commodity, 33, 37, 73, 77, 165
 control of, 27, 30, 43
 cost-based, 23
 gold, 146
 import, 76
 index of, 33, 54–5, 83
 real estate, 33
 relative, 134–5
 stability of, 125
 stabilization of, 100
 supports to, 37
productivity
 decline, 14, 89
 growth, 1, 3, 15, 16, 121, 132, 174, 176
 labour, 95, 167
profit
 rates, 87
 sharing, 34
protectionism, 45–6, 76, 105, 136–8

Recession
 costs of, 113
 1950s, 26
 1969–71, 27
 1970s, 2, 27, 32, 36, 168
 policy induced, 2, 27, 41, 43, 47–9, 87, 120, 168, 174
 victims of, 20
 world trade, 45–6
recovery
 agenda for, 54–5
 in Europe, 32
 non-inflationary, 12, 38, 54
 post-1974, 27, 32, 33
 prospects, 23, 156
redistribution of output, 114
restraint
 monetary, 47
 public sector, 50–1

Saudi Arabia, 154
shocks
 agricultural price, 42
 inflationary, 11, 20, 42, 54
 oil price, 2, 20, 42, 106, 133
 OPEC, 20
 supply, 28, 29, 42, 54–55
stagflation, 5, 15, 16, 20, 28, 30, 86–7, 90, 92, 105, 108–10, 132, 174, 175
stagnation, 16, 21, 38, 104, 174–5
subsidies, 87

Subject Index

Sweden
  balance of payments, 94, 99
  exchange rate, 94, 96, 98, 104, 140, 143
  GNP, 93, 99, 100
  indexing, 33
  inflation, 93, 168
  labour market, 93–94
  Long-Term Planning Commission, 99
  tax rates, 98
  trade balance, 145
  trade unions, 93
  unemployment, 92, 94
  wage guidelines, 17, 98
Swedish model, 93–4, 99, 101

tax
  incentives, 34, 38
  indirect, 33
  on unemployment compensation, 36
  US Code, 34
  on wages, 98
trade
  balance, 139, 140, 145–6
  balance ratio, 143–4
  deficit, 151
  and GATT, 46, 76, 136
  growth, 88, 104, 106
  management, 76
  restrictions, 45–6
  and stagnation, 87–8
  terms of, 33, 77, 132

unemployment
  classical, 27
  costs of, 15, 112
  cyclical, 115
  double digit, 157
  effects of, 10, 21, 121–2
  frictional, 7, 9, 37, 115, 127
  insurance, 27, 35, 36–7, 117, 159–60
  involuntary, 9, 14, 27, 29, 70, 115, 117
  and job vacancies, 27, 37
  and minimum wage, 36
  natural rate, 7, 26–7, 28, 29, 41, 46, 70, 118, 121, 139
  non-economic aspects, 126
  rates, 5, 16, 23, 26–7, 70, 96, 169
  search, 9, 169
  seasonal, 115
  structural, 7, 115
  voluntary, 7, 29, 72, 169
  and wage rates, 31
  youth, 21, 36
unions, 30, 32, 34–36, 93, 159, 160
United Kingdom (UK, Britain, England)
  deficit, 75
  exchange rate, 140, 143
  indexing, 55
  macroeconomic policy, 20, 30, 63
  monetary policy, 20, 30, 87
  output, 66
  structural imbalance, 75
  trade balance, 146
  unemployment, 23, 66, 70, 74, 77
United States
  Budget Office, 36
  controls, 30
  Council of Economic Advisors, 36
  CPI, 33
  deficit, 75, 151
  devaluation, 139, 140
  exchange rate, 140, 143, 145, 146
  Federal Reserve, 25–26, 41, 43, 56, 151
  fiscal policy, 44
  growth, 21
  inflation, 20, 23, 43
  interest rates, 24, 151
  job vacancy rates, 27
  macroeconomic policy, 20, 27, 63
  minimum wage, 36
  monetary policy, 20, 24–6, 87, 147
  structural imbalance, 75
  tax code, 34, 36
  trade balance, 146
  unemployment, 21, 23, 27, 116
  wage-setting, 31, 35, 36

velocity
  of M1, 43–4
  of M2, 44
  of monetary aggregates, 9–10
Versailles Conference, 147
Vietnam, 21, 26, 28

Wages
  asymmetrical response of, 28, 31, 34, 164
  bargaining, 48, 49, 52, 136
  concessions, 35
  controls, 27, 29–30, 38, 43, 54
  determination of, 69, 164
  guideposts, 38
  indexing of, 33
  inertia, 48, 49, 54, 120
  minimum, 35, 36, 118
  money, 120, 164
  real, 164
  relative, 35, 48, 124, 165
  setting mechanism, 29, 31–32, 35, 54, 56, 127
  in traded goods sector, 95

DATE DUE